The Pure Theory of International Trade

R. SHONE

Lecturer in Economic Statistics, University of Sheffield

Macmillan

First published 1972 by
THE MACMILLAN PRESS LTD
London and Basingstoke
Associated companies in New York Toronto
Dublin Melbourne Johannesburg and Madras

SBN 333 13341 2

Printed in Great Britain by
THE ANCHOR PRESS LTD
Tiptree, Essex

Editors' Preface to Macmillan Studies in Economics

The rapid growth of academic literature in the field of economics has posed serious problems for both students and teachers of the subject. The latter find it difficult to keep pace with more than a few areas of their subject so that an inevitable trend towards specialism emerges. The student quickly loses perspective as the maze of theories and models grows and the discipline accommodates an increasing amount of quantitative techniques

'Macmillan Studies in Economics' is a new series which sets out to provide the student with short, reasonably critical surveys of the developments within the various specialist areas of theoretical and applied economics. At the same time, the studies aim to form an integrated series so that, seen as a whole, they supply a balanced overview of the subject of economics. The emphasis in each study is upon recent work, but each topic will generally be placed in a historical context so that the reader may see the logical development of thought through time. Selected bibliographies are provided to guide readers to more extensive works. Each study aims at a brief treatment of the salient problems in order to avoid clouding the issues in detailed argument. Nonetheless, the texts are largely self-contained, and presume only that the student has some knowledge of elementary micro-economics and macro-economics.

Mathematical exposition has been adopted only where necessary. Some recent developments in economics are not readily comprehensible without some mathematics and statistics, and quantitative approaches also serve to shorten what would otherwise be lengthy and involved arguments. Where authors have found it necessary to introduce mathematical techniques, these techniques have been kept to a minimum. The emphasis is upon the economics, and not upon the quantitative methods. Later studies in the series will provide analyses of the links between quantitative methods, in particular econometrics, and economic analysis.

MACMILLAN STUDIES IN ECONOMICS

General Editors: D. C. ROWAN and G. R. FISHER

Executive Editor: D. W. PEARCE

Contents

Preface and Acknowledgements

This book is not an exposition of trade theory; it is an account of the literature on international trade theory: these two should not be confused. The aim has been to write a book which gives the undergraduate specialist in international trade a guided tour of what the trade experts have said about problems of international trade. With the ready reprint of many trade articles it is now apparent that the student requires a sifting process and a means of seeing the literature in perspective. It is this purpose to which this book is directed and, it is hoped, which it fulfils.

I am indebted to Dr George McKenzie of the University of Washington at St Louis, to Professor Ivor Pearce of the University of Southampton, and to M. Steuer of the London School of Economics for comments on an earlier draft of this book. Their suggestions proved invaluable, but I alone am responsible for any remaining errors.

R. S.

1 Introduction

The pure theory of international trade is concerned with the fundamental relationships which exist between two trading bodies. In one sense it is a branch of exchange theory, but because the exchanging bodies are, on the whole, countries, additional relationships come into play. It was often debated in the past – although the distinction is readily accepted today – as to why we should have a theory of international trade, i.e. whether there is a distinction between inter-regional trade and international trade. The usual reasons given for distinguishing the two are: (i) international immobility of factors of production; (ii) independent monetary systems; (iii) the existence of political boundaries and controls which go with them; and (iv) greater geographical differences and greater transport costs. However, each of these is a matter of degree only.

Given, therefore, that one considers it important to have a theory of international trade, we shall be considering in this essay to what extent and in what way economists have gone about accounting for the pattern of trade. The questions to be answered are, for example:

1. What goods enter into international trade?
2. Why does a country carry on trade with another?
3. What is the level of a country's trade?
4. On what terms does a country trade?
5. What effects do growth, factor distortions, tariffs, quotas, etc., have on the volume and terms of trade?

These are just some of the questions to which trade theorists have attempted to supply an answer.

Analytically, trade theory began with David Ricardo's theory of comparative advantage, which is taken up in Section 2. This was the first and simplest general equilibrium analysis which combined two countries, two commodities, one factor, and its return. Although this particular model has been abandoned, or more correctly absorbed, into more elaborate models such as

11

the Heckscher–Ohlin model outlined in Section 3, the general equilibrium framework has remained in preference to Marshallian partial equilibrium analysis. This is one of the distinctions between the pure theory of trade and its monetary counterpart, which uses more readily the partial equilibrium analysis. Furthermore, the general equilibrium models employed tend to be non-operational, but still serve the purpose of setting out the logic and consistency of a system which is a conceptualisation of the real world.

The procedure adopted by most authors is to set up a logically consistent model and establish firstly whether an equilibrium solution exists. The next consideration is the uniqueness of the equilibrium – a question raised very early on by J. S. Mill. Having established these, a comparative static exercise is carried out. That is to say, one of the variables originally considered as constant is allowed to change and the system is left to settle down at a new equilibrium, this new equilibrium then being compared with the old. This should be borne in mind when reading Sections 3–6, which consist of nothing but comparative statics.

The student must also constantly bear in mind the distinction between positive and normative economics. The former is concerned with *what is* whilst the latter is concerned with *what ought* to be. This is particularly true when considering the gains from trade (Section 5) and the effects of government policy on trade (Section 6).

Throughout this essay a consistent notation will be used. For ease of reference we shall summarise it here. S_i and X_i denote the supply and demand for the ith commodity respectively; the price of the ith commodity is given by q_i. A_{ij} denotes the input of the jth factor in the production of the ith commodity, and $a_{ij} \equiv A_{ij}/S_i$; the price of the jth factor is given by p_j. A_j denotes the endowment of the jth factor, i.e. $A_j = \sum_i A_{ij}$. All terms so far listed without a prime will refer to country I, whilst terms accompanied with primes refer to country II. For example, q_2/q_1 is the domestic (country I's) price ratio, and q'_2/q'_1 is the price ratio in country II. In addition, MRS refers to the marginal rate of substitution in consumption, i.e. the slope of the indifference curve, and MRT refers to the marginal rate of transformation, i.e. the slope of the production possibility boundary.

12

2 Comparative Advantage

In 1776 Adam Smith argued that if a country could produce a good cheaper than a second country, and if the second country could produce a different good more cheaply than the first, it would be to the advantage of both countries if they specialised in the good they could produce cheapest, and traded. For example, the tropics are more suited to growing bananas than the temperate zone and with the same amount of labour the tropics can produce far more bananas than can the U.K. On the other hand the U.K. is more suited to producing machine goods and with the same amount of labour the U.K. can produce more machinery than can a tropical country. It will be of obvious advantage to both countries to employ the division of labour and to produce the good in which each has an *absolute* advantage and undertake international exchange. The qualification 'absolute' is necessary because the question arises, as Torrens and Ricardo pointed out:[1] what if a country can produce both goods in greater amount with the same labour as a second country – will trade cease under these circumstances? Ricardo argued that under these conditions it would be to the (possible) advantage of both countries if they specialised in the good in which they had a *comparative* advantage.

We can illustrate the distinction between absolute and comparative advantage by considering the Ricardian model a little more carefully. At the same time we can introduce some useful analytical tools which will be helpful in considering other aspects of trade theory. Ricardian theory is based on the *labour theory of value*. This theory considers labour to be the only means of production, the value and output being determined by the labour content required in the production of each good. Fig. 1 illustrates the important features of the theory. A country possesses a total endowment of labour, A_1. If it uses all this

[1] R. Torrens, *The Economists Refuted* (1808), and D. Ricardo, *Principles of Political Economy* (1817) chap. 7.

13

labour in the production of good 1 it produces a maximum output of S^*_1. On the other hand if it employs all its labour in the production of good 2 it produces S^*_2. If it employs only some of its labour to produce good 1, namely A_{11}, it will produce only S_1 ($< S^*_1$) as shown in Fig. 1(a). The remaining labour, A_{21} ($= A_1 - A_{11}$), is used to produce S_2 ($< S^*_2$). Two points are worth noting: (i) The rays through the origin denote the production functions in this Ricardian model because they show the relationship which exists between the input of labour and the resultant output. The fact that each good employs labour in a different proportion means that the production

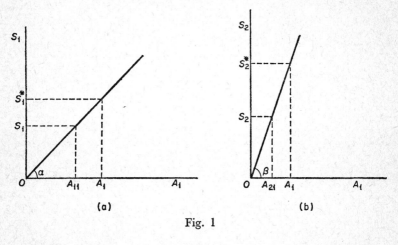

(a)   (b)

Fig. 1

functions are different. (ii) The production functions are linear. Linearity arises because each commodity uses labour (the only input) in a fixed proportion: in other words, twice as much output requires twice as much labour.

We can represent the combinations of S_1 and S_2 open to the community by considering the production possibility set. The maxima of S_1 and S_2 have already been established and so these can be marked off in Fig. 2. Consider the slope S^*_1/S^*_2. We have already defined $a_{ij} = A_{ij}/S_i$, so we have from Fig. 1 $S_1/A_{11} = a = 1/a_{11}$ and $S_2/A_{21} = \beta = 1/a_{21}$. It follows then that $S^*_1/S^*_2 = aA_1/\beta A_1 = a/\beta = a_{21}/a_{11}$. But what does this ratio mean in the present model? The cost of producing a unit of each commodity is the wage rate multiplied by the amount of labour required to produce a unit of output, i.e. p_1a_{11} and p_2a_{21} for goods 1 and 2 respectively, where p_1 and p_2 denote the wage rate in each industry. But under perfect competition wage rates are equalised and so the labour cost of good 1 is $q_1 = pa_{11}$ and for good 2 is $q_2 = pa_{21}$. The ratio of unit cost is $q_2/q_1 = pa_{21}/pa_{11} = a_{21}/a_{11}$, and this ratio holds irrespective of demand. It follows, therefore, that no matter what the level of production of S_1 and S_2 they will always lie on the straight line joining S^*_1 and S^*_2.

Now all that has been said applies only to country I. What is the situation in country II? Ricardo assumed that each country employed labour in a different proportion in the production of the same good. In other words, country II

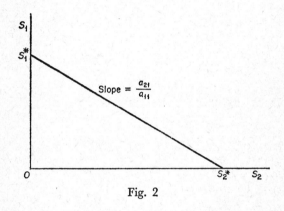

Fig. 2

produced S'_1 by employing labour in a proportion different from a, say a'. Similarly, commodity 2 employed labour in a proportion different from β, say β'. For country II, therefore, the production possibility boundary has a slope a'_{21}/a'_{11}, which by the same reasoning of the last paragraph is the relative labour costs of the two commodities, i.e. $q'_2/q'_1 = a'_{21}/a'_{11}$.

Consider, then, the two alternative situations depicted in Fig. 3. OAB represents the production set for country I and OCD the production set for country II.

The production possibility boundary AB has slope a_{21}/a_{11} (relative to the horizontal axis), and the production possibility boundary CD has slope a'_{21}/a'_{11}. It is clear from Fig. 3(a) that if each country uses all its labour, A, to produce commodity 1, then more can be produced by country I. On the other hand, if both countries attempt to produce the second commodity,

15

country II would produce more than country I. Clearly, country I has an absolute advantage in the production of S_1 and country II has an absolute advantage in the production of S_2.

Fig. 3(*b*) shows the situation put forward by Ricardo and Torrens, namely, country II being able to produce more of both goods than country I. In other words country II has an absolute advantage in the production of both goods. But as the slope AD' (parallel to CD) reveals, country II has a comparative advantage in the production of commodity 2, this is because if it gives up resources sufficient to produce OA of commodity 1 it can produce OD' ($>OB$) of good 2. On the other hand if it gave up resources used to produce OB of good 2 it would only

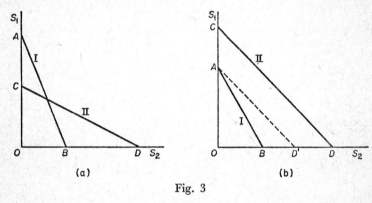

Fig. 3

be able to produce good 1 by an amount less than OA. We have the situation, then, that if $a_{21}/a_{11} > a'_{21}/a'_{11}$ country I has a comparative advantage in the production of good 1 and country II has a comparative advantage in the production of good 2. So long as these comparative cost ratios differ, both countries have the possibility of gaining if each country specialises in the good for which its relative cost ratio is least. The reason for this is that, having specialised, the ratio at which each country trades internationally is no worse, but probably better, than the domestic cost ratio.

Ricardian theory assumes (i) that although factors are mobile domestically they are immobile internationally. (ii) It is, in its original formulation, dependent upon the labour theory of value. (iii) There are only two countries and two commodities. (iv) Unit costs are constant. The development of the literature after Ricardo was largely directed at demonstrating that some of these conditions were not necessary, and that others could be generalised without any substantial change in the conclusion of the theory, namely:

P.1. A country will export a good in which it has a comparative advantage and import a good for which it has a comparative disadvantage.

Haberler [10] gives a clear discussion of each of these assumptions, and in particular demonstrates that the labour theory of value is not necessary for a statement of the comparative cost doctrine. Earlier writers such as Bastable and Marshall attempted to replace 'labour costs' by 'real costs', but these attempts were superseded by Haberler's concept of opportunity cost ([10] chap. 12). This formulation states that the cost of a commodity is the amount of another commodity forgone. Under perfect competition this is the ratio of marginal costs (and furthermore, marginal private and social costs are assumed to coincide). In the Ricardian model marginal costs are pa_{11} and pa_{21} and so the ratio of marginal costs gives the same result. However, a generalisation to more factor inputs still allows the computation of marginal costs and the ratio obtained for the two commodities. In the present model, since marginal costs are constant for both commodities whatever the level of production, the ratio of marginal costs is also constant. In other words, the production possibility boundary is a straight line, the slope of which represents the country's comparative cost ratio. The same is true for the second country, the commodities there establishing a production possibility boundary which is also linear and whose slope represents its comparative cost ratio.[1]

In replacing the labour cost doctrine by that of opportunity cost, Haberler demonstrated that there is an increasing cost in giving up more and more of one commodity in order to

[1] An exposition of the relationship between marginal costs and opportunity cost will be found in R. G. Lipsey, *An Introduction to Positive Economics*, 2nd ed. (London, Weidenfeld & Nicolson, 1967) appendix to chap. 52. He there proves the following proposition:

P. The opportunity cost of good 2 in terms of good 1 is equal to the ratio of the marginal cost of good 2 to that of good 1, which in turn is equal to the ratio of the commodity price of good 1 to that of good 2.

17

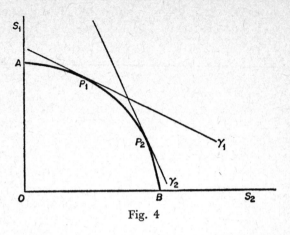

Fig. 4

produce another. As most elementary textbooks now show, the production possibility curve is concave to the origin as shown in Fig. 4. Under these circumstances the opportunity cost, which denotes the ratio of marginal costs or the commodity price ratio, varies according to the production combination chosen by the economy. If, before trade, the country produced at point P_1 then the comparative cost ratio is given by γ_1. If, however, it produced the commodity bundle P_2, then the comparative cost ratio would be γ_2 ($> \gamma_1$ relative to the horizontal axis). The same situation holds for country II, the production set there giving rise to a comparative cost ratio γ' say. So long as these comparative cost ratios differ the Ricardian analysis holds good.

Ricardo did not in fact demonstrate at what terms trade would take place. If the terms were country I's cost ratio, country II would obtain all the benefit; if trade took place at country II's price ratio, then country I would obtain all the benefit from trade. But the question not faced by Ricardo was: what determines the terms on which two countries trade with one another, i.e. what determines the terms of trade? This question was answered by J. S. Mill and elaborated by A. Marshall and F. Y. Edgeworth.[1] Both Marshall and Edgeworth employed a graphical technique to demonstrate the determina-

[1] J. S. Mill, *Principles of Political Economy* (1848), bk III, chap 18; *Essays on Some Unsettled Questions of Political Economy* (1864), essay I; A. Marshall, *The Pure Theory of Foreign Trade* (1879); F. Y. Edgeworth, *The Theory of International Values* (1894).

tion of the equilibrium terms of trade. Marshall constructed a curve which established for each price ratio between two countries the amount of the commodity country I is willing to offer in exchange for imports. This he called a *reciprocal demand curve*, or *offer curve*. A similar offer curve is constructed for country II. These curves reflect each country's demand for the other country's good. It is apparent in this that Ricardo, in ignoring the terms on which trade took place, constructed a supply theory of international trade. The demand side was supplied by Marshall and Edgeworth.

Demand has always raised a problem in trade literature because it is the community's demand that must be considered. In order to pursue problems in trade a community indifference curve was introduced into the literature by Leontief [25]. These curves have similar properties to individual indifference curves in that (i) they are convex to the origin, (ii) the further from the origin the greater the welfare, and (iii) they indicate an ordinal ranking, i.e. the amount by which welfare is greater as one moves to a higher indifference curve cannot be assessed. We have therefore the following proposition.:

P.2. A community indifference curve depicts all commodity combinations that will yield constant utility to the members of the community – individually and together.

Put simply, if a community consisted of two individuals (or groups) then the community indifference curve is established by varying the combination of goods in such a manner that both individuals remain indifferent simultaneously. However, the community indifference curves are established under a fixed distribution of income. If this distribution alters – in particular if the trade policy alters the distribution – then a new set of community indifference curves must be established, i.e. to each income distribution there is associated an indifference map or, alternatively, the community's indifference map is not independent of the country's income distribution.

Country I's demand pattern along with that of country II is shown in Fig. 5; also represented are the production sets. The demands of each country are embodied in their community indifference curves, illustrated by i_1 and i_2 for country I, and i'_1 and i'_2 for country II.

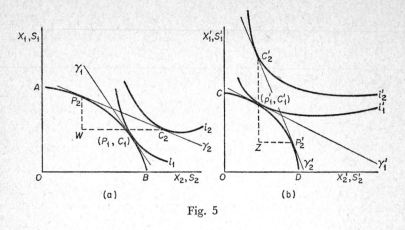

Fig. 5

Now that we possess both demand and supply we can consider a country's closed economy equilibrium, i.e. its equilibrium in the absence of trade. Just as for the individual, the community is in equilibrium (on the consumption side) when its price ratio is equal to the marginal rate of substitution (MRS) i.e. the slope of the indifference curve. Production is in equilibrium when the price ratio is equal to the marginal rate of transformation, i.e. the slope of the production possibility boundary. All-round equilibrium will only be satisfied where:

$$\text{MRS}_I = q_2/q_1 = \text{MRT}_I$$
$$\text{MRS}_{II} = q'_2/q'_1 = \text{MRT}_{II} \tag{1}$$

As can be seen in Fig. 5, at a comparative cost ratio γ_1, with production and consumption at (P_1, C_1) country I is in equilibrium; similarly for country II at (P'_1, C'_1) at a price ratio γ'_1.

Since in the closed-economy equilibrium $\gamma_1 > \gamma'_1$, in other words $a_{21}/a_{11} > a'_{21}/a'_{11}$, then country I has a comparative advantage in the production of S_1 and country II in S'_2. Each country, therefore, increases its production of the good in which it has a comparative advantage, country I moving to P_2 on its production boundary AB, and country II moving to P'_2 on its production boundary CD.

The act of trading moves country I further along AB towards A and so decreases the price ratio, as shown in Fig. 5 by $\gamma_2 < \gamma_1$. At the new price ratio, γ_2, production of commodity 1 exceeds domestic consumption and so the remainder $x_1 (= S_1 - X_1)$ can be offered for exports. On the other hand,

20

country II has moved along CD towards D and at γ'_2 its home production of good 2 exceeds home demand, and country II wishes to import $x'_1 = X'_1 - S'_1$. We can exhibit these offers of exports and demand for imports on a separate diagram as shown in Fig. 6.

At the closed-economy price ratios γ_1 and γ'_1 nothing is offered for trade, but as can be seen from Fig. 6 the divergence between the comparative cost ratios is greatest and the potential gain from trade is at a maximum. At a price ratio γ_2

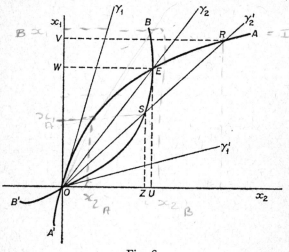

Fig. 6

country I offers P_2W ($=OW$ in Fig. 6) and demands WC_2 ($=WE$). The curve $A'OA$ therefore denotes country I's demand for country II's good at various commodity price ratios, or terms on which trade is carried on. At γ'_2 country II is willing to offer OZ in exchange for SZ of good 1. Thus $B'OB$ represents country II's demand for country I's good. The curves $A'OA$ and $B'OB$ are the offer curves of Marshall and Edgeworth. It should be apparent that the south-west quadrant denotes the desire of country I to import good 1 (rather than export as in the north-east quadrant) and export good 2, and for country II to export good 1 and import good 2 (whilst importing good 1 and exporting good 2 in the north-east quadrant).

Consider for a moment the price ratio (terms of trade) which rules internationally as being γ'_2 – remember that only one ratio can hold which is the same for both countries. If we consider that all demands are realised so that points R on OA and S on OB are the relevant indicators, then by reading off what is demanded of good 1 by country II, viz. SZ, and what is supplied by country I, viz. OV, it is apparent that there is an excess supply of good 1. It can also be established by suitable reading of Fig. 6 that good 2 is in excess demand, $VR > OZ$. This will almost certainly mean the price of good 1 will fall internationally and that of good 2 will rise. But $\gamma = q_2/q_1$ which means that this ratio will rise and so the terms of trade will move to the left towards OE. In fact it is readily established that at a price ratio to the left of OE there will be an excess demand for good 1 and an excess supply of good 2, and the result will be a rightward movement towards OE. Only at OE is there no excess demand or supply. It follows that the equilibrium terms at which both countries are willing to trade is that price ratio at which the amount country I is willing to offer in exchange for country II's good is equal to the amount country II is willing to offer in exchange for country I's good, viz. OE in Fig. 6.

In equilibrium the triangle OWE is the same as the triangle OEU in Fig. 6; in terms of Fig. 5, if we consider $\gamma_2 = \gamma'_2$ to be the equilibrium terms of trade OE, then P_2WC_2 is the same as $P'_2ZC'_2$ which means that the amount country I exports of good 1 is exactly equal to the amount country II wishes to import, and similarly for good 2. In equilibrium, therefore, both countries face the same international terms of trade, and this ratio is the same as the MRS in consumption and the MRT in production in *both* countries. We have in equilibrium:

$$\mathrm{MRS_I} = \mathrm{MRT_I} = \frac{q'_2}{q'_1} = \mathrm{MRS_{II}} = \mathrm{MRT_{II}}. \tag{2}$$

Consider once again Fig. 3(b). Suppose the offer curves OA and OB were such that the terms of trade were the same as country II's comparative cost ratio (in this case OA would be a straight line through the origin so that the equilibrium terms of trade remained the same no matter how OB shifted), and let this be given by CD' (parallel to CD) in Fig. 3(b). Then in the Ricardian model country I would specialise in the production of S_1 and country II would produce some of both

22

goods. In the Ricardian model, therefore, the offer curves would consist only of a country's demand response for the other country's good. But consider the derivation of the offer curves from Fig. 5; there is both a demand response as the economy moves from C_1 to C_2 and a supply response as the economy moves along its production possibility boundary from P_1 to P_2. In other words the offer curve, although referred to as a reciprocal demand curve, embodies *both* demand and supply responses on the part of a trading country. This modern version of comparative costs has been outlined by many authors (e.g. [16], [20], [21], [23] and [28]).

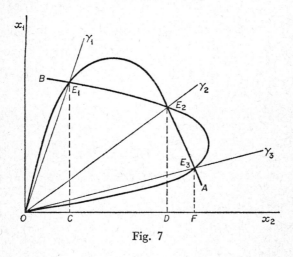

Fig. 7

Having demonstrated that an equilibrium terms of trade exists, the literature has focused on two issues stemming from this. The first is concerned with the uniqueness of equilibrium; the second with the stability of equilibrium. Fig. 7 shows the situation where more than one equilibrium terms of trade exists, viz. γ_1, γ_2, γ_3. The volumes of trade associated with E_1, E_2 and E_3 are clearly different as indicated by the triangles OE_1C, OE_2D and OE_3F, the sides of which denote exports and imports. Corresponding to each level of trade volume there is a different internal situation; that is to say, the domestic economy will have a different production and consumption pattern, a different level of money supply and demand, and a different level of investment, besides different distributions of each of

23

these for E_1, E_2 and E_3. Therefore, there will be a different level of welfare associated with each equilibrium. Can one conclude that the greater the volume of trade the greater a country's welfare? As we shall indicate in this essay, we cannot necessarily conclude that this is true.

A unique equilibrium as drawn in Fig. 6 will occur if both goods are normal in trade, i.e. a favourable movement in the terms of trade is associated with an increased offer of exportables and an increased demand for importables. A necessary, although not sufficient, condition for multiple equilibria is that at least one good is inferior in trade. This is illustrated in Fig. 7. A movement in the terms of trade from γ_1 to γ_2 denotes a favourable movement for country I in that for the same exports of good 1 it obtains more imports of good 2; and conversely it represents an unfavourable movement from country II's point of view. Country II, however, although it offers more of good 2, demands less of good 1 in return. Hence good 1 is inferior in trade and it is this condition which means that the offer curves OA and OB are likely to intersect more than once.

Discussion of international stability has been prominent in the literature.[1] The problem is sometimes put in terms of static and dynamic stability, the former referring to the shapes of the static offer curves, the latter to the type of dynamic adjustment mechanism specified. Behind the static stability lies the adjustment mechanism that price will rise when there is excess demand and fall when there is excess supply, all taking place in the single time period – a period which is representative and can be considered in isolation. For example, in Fig. 6 at terms of trade γ'_2 there is a disequilibrium on the balance of

---

[1] It was discussed by Marshall in his *Pure Theory of Foreign Trade* (1879) and was given a mathematical treatment by P. A. Samuelson in his *Foundations of Economic Analysis* (Harvard U.P., Cambridge, Mass.; Oxford U.P., 1947) pp. 266–8. As Samuelson's equations testify (eq. (25), p. 266) and Kemp's treatment shows ([22] chap. 5), Marshall's adjustment equations relate the actual offers over time as a function of the divergence between actual and equilibrium offers. An alternative dynamic adjustment, and one most common in modern literature, relates the change in the terms of trade over time as a function of the actual less the equilibrium terms of trade (e.g. [32]). The former is a quantity adjustment, the latter a price adjustment mechanism.

trade because of an excess demand for good 2 and an excess supply of good 1. The price of importables will therefore rise and the price of exportables will fall resulting in the terms of trade moving towards OE. For any price ratio to the left of γ_2 a price adjustment will occur that will bring the terms of trade to OE. Under these conditions we say that E is statically stable. But consider E_2 in Fig. 7. For terms of trade to the right of γ_2 there is an excess demand for good 1 and an excess supply of good 2 (the student is advised to sketch this himself). The price adjustment mechanism causes q_1 to rise and q_2 to fall, which means that the ratio q_2/q_1 falls and the terms of trade move away from OE_2 towards OE_3. It can be found in an exactly analogous manner that for terms of trade to the left of OE_2 the price adjustment mechanism will cause the terms of trade to move away from OE_2 and towards OE_1. In other words, E_2 is an unstable equilibrium. It is apparent that static instability is very much connected with the shape of the offer curves.

Dynamic stability or instability arises from specifying an adjustment mechanism over time which links one period with the next. For example, in the initial disequilibrium state excess demands are met out of stocks and excess supplies by additions to stocks. In the following period price adjustments are made according to the pressures from existing stock levels ([35] chap. 3). If the price adjustment to the change in stock levels overshoots the equilibrium, the disequilibrium may worsen. This may then turn the statically stable equilibrium of Fig. 6 into one which is dynamically unstable. Or alternatively it may result in the statically unstable equilibrium E_2 in Fig. 7 exhibiting dynamic stability in that the disequilibrium *over time* decreases.

Static stability and instability have been given emphasis in the literature because of their association with the Marshall–Lerner condition. This sets out the conditions under which a devaluation (revaluation) will correct a balance of payments deficit (surplus). From a purely theoretical point of view interest is centred on the way in which the terms of trade must move to correct a deficit or surplus. The movement in the terms of trade may or may not be carried out by means of a devaluation (revaluation). Given a deficit (surplus), a rise (fall) in the price of imports relative to exports will correct a deficit (surplus) only if the offer curves are exhibiting static stability, for example in the neighbourhood of γ_1 and γ_3 in Fig. 7. If the shape of the offer curves is such that the terms of trade were in the neighbourhood of an unstable equilibrium such as γ_2, then such a movement in the terms of trade would increase rather than decrease the deficit (surplus). In terms of elasticities, the Marshall–Lerner condition states:

P.3. If the absolute value of the elasticity of demand for imports by the home country plus the elasticity of demand for imports by the foreign country exceeds unity, equilibrium is stable and an unfavourable (favourable) movement in the terms of trade will correct a deficit (surplus).[1]

This is outlined, for example, by Mundell ([32] (1968) p. 13) and Kemp ([22] chap. 5). But it must be emphasised that many assumptions have been made in stating the stability condition in this simplified form ([35] pp. 63–4).

Uniqueness and stability have not been the only considerations given to the analysis of comparative costs. The case where there are more than two commodities but still two countries and only one factor of production has also been given attention. We have established that if $a_{21}/a_{11} > a'_{21}/a'_{11}$ then country I has a comparative advantage in good 1 and country II in good 2 (see Fig. 3). This expression can equally be written $a'_{11}/a_{11} > a'_{21}/a_{21}$, and this shows that the relative cost of producing good 1 is cheaper for country I than for country II. Now suppose we have n commodities so that we can obtain all the ratios a'_{i1}/a_{i1} $(i = 1, \ldots n)$. Suppose we rank all these ratios from the largest to the smallest as follows: $a'_{11}/a_{11} > a'_{21}/a_{21} > \ldots > a'_{n1}/a_{n1}$. The question arises: in which of these

---

[1] Proposition 3 is in many respects misleading because to state it in this way normally means that 'total' elasticities or excess demand elasticities are introduced. In doing this the elasticities no longer take on the property of being a parameter of the model – and hence constant – which is the whole point of their introduction. Only 'partial' elasticities make any sense. The importance of this distinction with reference to the stability/instability problem in the balance of payments was first put forward by I. F. Pearce in his article, 'The Problem of the Balance of Payments', *International Economic Review*, II (1961) 1–28.

goods has country I a comparative advantage such that it is likely to export that good, and in which has it a comparative disadvantage such that it is likely to import it?

A country will import a good if the foreign price – converted at the ruling exchange rate – is cheaper than the domestic price. Let e represent the price of foreign currency in terms of domestic currency, e.g. let the domestic currency be pounds sterling and the foreign currency dollars, then $e = \pounds x/\$1$. Country I, the domestic economy, will export good 1 if $q_1 < eq'_1$, because to the foreign country the dollar price of country I's good, viz. q_1/e, is smaller than their own dollar price q'_1. But consider what this means in terms of the wage rates p and p' at home and abroad. Using the fact that $q_1 = pa_{11}$ and $q'_1 = p'a'_{11}$, we have by substitution:

$$\frac{p}{ep'} > \frac{a'_{11}}{a_{11}} \tag{3}$$

On the other hand, if $q_2 > eq'_2$ country I will import good 2 and this implies:

$$\frac{p}{ep'} > \frac{a'_{21}}{a_{21}} \tag{4}$$

Combining these two results we see that a country will import all goods satisfying inequality (4) and export all goods satisfying inequality (3); but this is no more than $a'_{11}/a_{11} > a'_{21}/a_{21}$ which we indicated above as denoting country I's comparative advantage in good 1 and country II's comparative advantage in good 2. But now we have introduced an additional condition which can be used in considering the array of n goods. All we need to do is establish the ratio p/ep'. This is done by imposing the condition that the balance of payments must be in equilibrium, say at terms of trade OE in Fig. 6. At this equilibrium there will be a unique set (p, p', e) of wage rates and exchange rate. From this the ratio p/ep' is calculated. Then for all $a'_{i1}/a_{i1} < p/ep'$ commodity i is imported into country I, for all $a'_{k1}/a_{k1} > p/ep'$ commodity k is exported by the home country, and where $a'_{s1}/a_{s1} = p/ep'$ commodity s is not traded (or, strictly, no benefit or loss will arise by trading this good).

A disturbance to the equilibrium balance of payments will cause a change in one or more of p, p' and e. The adjustment mechanism will re-establish equilibrium in the balance of payments. This will be at a new ratio p/ep', and hence with a different set of goods imported and exported. It will be noted, that as in the two-commodity model, the ranking of the comparative factor productivity ratios is independent of demand; however, the precise break in the chain, which divides the goods into those imported and those exported, is dependent on demand. This argument was first established by Mangoldt, was summarised and developed in English by Edgeworth, and was later elaborated by Viner and Haberler [10].

The introduction of transport costs does not materially affect the conclusions of the comparative cost doctrine. In the two-good two-country model it narrows the margin of divergence between comparative cost ratios; and in the many-good model it alters the point of demarcation and creates a zone of goods which are non-traded because of transport costs [10]. Also, an increase in the number of countries does not materially affect the conclusions, as Jones has demonstrated [21].

3 The Heckscher–Ohlin Theorem and the Theorem of Factor Price Equalisation

HECKSCHER–OHLIN MODEL

The Ricardian theory of comparative costs and the introduction of the terms of trade explains to a certain degree why trade occurs, in what commodities, and its volume. But it does not give any account as to *why* comparative cost ratios differ between countries. One answer to this question was supplied by Heckscher in 1919 [12] and elaborated by his pupil Ohlin [34]. Their approach has been formally worked out by later economists, e.g. Johnson [16], Jones [20], Lancaster [23] and Stolper and Samuelson [44], and the Heckscher–Ohlin model, as it has become known, is the foundation of most pure trade theory.

The Heckscher–Ohlin (H–O) theorem can be stated as follows:

P.4. A country will export those commodities in which its most abundant factor is used relatively intensively and import those commodities which incorporate the factors with which it is least endowed.

In other words, different initial endowments of factors of production give rise to differences in comparative costs, which in turn give rise to trade. In deriving this theorem a number of assumptions must be made:

(i) The theorem, initially, is concerned with two countries, two commodities and two factors, i.e. a $2 \times 2 \times 2$ model.

(ii) In the Ricardian model, production functions were

different in the two countries for the same commodity. Heckscher and Ohlin argued that production functions are the *same* everywhere.[1] This assumption of identity of production functions has been retained in most treatments of the theory.

(iii) The production functions are linearly homogeneous.

(iv) It is assumed that factors, although mobile domestically, are completely immobile internationally.

(v) Perfect competition prevails in all markets, this ensures that (*a*) all factors are fully employed, (*b*) factors are paid according to their marginal product, and (*c*) commodities are priced at marginal cost.

(vi) Factor reversal is excluded (see p. 36 below), and neither country specialises either before or after trade.

(vii) Heckscher and Ohlin assumed that consumption patterns are similar.

Although the list of assumptions is long, this in itself is not a criticism of the theory. What matters is to what extent the assumptions are unlikely to be fulfilled, and the sensitivity of the theorem to a violation of one or more of its assumptions.

In establishing the validity of the H–O theory many new techniques of analysis have been introduced. The Edgeworth–Bowley box has been employed to analyse the factor and production sides ever since Stolper and Samuelson showed its usefulness [44]. The production possibility boundary, domestic commodity price ratio, offer curves and the terms of trade have been combined in an analytical technique of general equilibrium analysis to illustrate a country's comparative advantage and the volume of trade – a technique considered fairly comprehensively by Meade [28]. Mathematical formulations are not lacking either, e.g. Kemp [22] and Pearce [35].[2] We shall here consider some of these developments.

---

[1] The identical production functions assumption has been opposed by some writers, e.g. S. B. Linder in his *An Essay on Trade and Transformation* (Wiley, New York and London, 1961); but it has recently been defended ([35] chap. 12).

[2] For a survey of the mathematical developments the student may consult J. S. Chipman, 'A Survey of the Theory of International Trade: Part 3, The Modern Theory', *Econometrica*, xxxiv (1966) 685–760.

What must first be established is the relationship which exists between a country's factor endowment and its production set. As mentioned above, the H–O theorem considers an economy which has two basic factors of production, A_1 and A_2. These endowments are fixed throughout the whole of the analysis. We can represent these endowments as the sides of a box as illustrated in Fig. 8(a). O_1A_1 denotes the total endowment of factor 1 possessed by country I and O_1A_2 represents the total endowment of factor 2. Any point in the box represents various feasible combinations of the country's endowment; a point north-east, say, of O_2 is not feasible because it means a factor

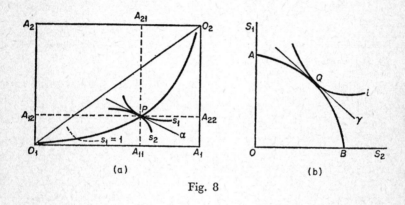

(a)   (b)

Fig. 8

endowment of A_1 and/or A_2 which exceeds what the country possesses.

In this model both inputs are employed to produce commodity S_1, but they can be employed in varying combinations. For example, consider the curve denoted $s_1 = 1$. This indicates various combinations of factors A_1 and A_2 that can be combined to produce one unit of S_1. In other words, a unit of S_1 can be produced with much of A_1 and little of A_2 or by a little of A_1 and a large amount of A_2. This curve is called an isoquant, and $s_1 = 1$ is the unit isoquant. The assumption that the production functions are linearly homogeneous means that every other isoquant is just like $s_1 = 1$ but is further from the origin O_1 and denotes a greater output. The isoquant Ps_1 is the same shape as $s_1 = 1$ but denotes a greater production of commodity 1.

In this model the economy also wishes to produce good 2 and to do this it must also employ some of its factor endowments

A_1 and A_2. The production conditions for commodity 2, however, have O_2 as the origin and the employment of factors A_1 and A_2 are read off from this origin. Just as for the first commodity, the production conditions are embodied in the isoquants of which Ps_2 is representative.

From this information we should be able to establish how much of each commodity is produced and how the country's endowment of factors is distributed between the two commodities. Consider point P. This lies on isoquants Ps_1 and Ps_2 simultaneously. We see from Fig. 8(a) that at this point the production of this quantity of S_1 uses A_{11} of factor 1 and A_{12} of factor 2. On the other hand, the production of S_2 represented by point P on Ps_2 uses up A_{21} of factor 1 and A_{22} of factor 2. We see that a point such as this where the two isoquants are tangential that the economy fully employs its factors the production of both commodities, for $A_{11} + A_{12} = A_1$ and in $A_{21} + A_{22} = A_2$.

The theory assumes perfect competition in all markets – assumption (v) above. A result of this is that the economy must always be at a point such as P where the isoquants are tangential, for only then will all the factors be fully employed. There is an infinity of such points and they lie on a curve such as O_1PO_2, which is referred to as the efficiency locus (or sometimes the contract curve).

Consider for a moment the situation when the economy uses all its factor endowments to produce commodity 1. This quantity would be obtained from the isoquant for good 1 which passes through the point O_2. This amount is marked off in Fig. 8(b) as the distance OA on the vertical axis. The economy could alternatively produce nothing of good 1 and use all its factors in the production of good 2. This amount is obtained from the isoquant for good 2 which passes through O_1 and is the distance OB on the horizontal axis in Fig. 8(b). But we know that all the production combinations which arise from a full-employment situation lie on the efficiency locus O_1PO_2, and so the output combinations of point P – being the outputs of the isoquants passing through P – can also be marked off in Fig. 8(b). Here point Q in the $S_1 - S_2$ plane corresponds to point P in the $A_1 - A_2$ plane. In other words, the efficiency locus can be transformed into the production possibility boundary AB: to each point on the efficiency locus there corresponds a unique point on the production possibility boundary. How this is performed geometrically is outlined by Savosnick [42].

If demand and supply are in equilibrium at point Q, then we can ascertain from Fig. 8(a) the distribution of the factors because of the unique correspondence between P and Q. But can we take the analysis any further: can we not associate in some way the prices of the factors and the commodity prices embodied in the line $\gamma = q_2/q_1$? From the theory of the firm we know that the line a in Fig. 8(a) represents the factor price ratio p_2/p_1.[1] Since a is uniquely determined at point P, there is a one-to-one correspondence between the commodity price ratio at point Q and the factor price ratio at P.

The Edgeworth–Bowley box, as it is called, was introduced into trade literature by Stolper and Samuelson [44]. Its value is in being able to represent six variables simultaneously: S_1, S_2, A_1, A_2, p_1 and p_2, i.e. outputs as represented by the isoquants; factor endowments, which fix the dimension of the box; and factor prices, whose ratio is represented by the slope of the isoquant. A similar box exists for country II and the same set of relationships can be established. But to a large extent this is unnecessary because in the present model it is assumed that production functions are the same the world over. The only difference lies in (i) the factor endowments, and hence the size of the Edgeworth–Bowley box for country II, (ii) the resultant production set, and, unless assumed to the contrary, (iii) different indifference maps denoting different demand patterns.

Before leaving this analysis it is useful to introduce another type of diagram which illustrates the relationship, referred to above, between factor price ratios and commodity price ratios. In doing this we shall also bring all the analysis together to illustrate the effect of trade.

Fig. 9 is a redrawing of Fig. 8 showing the situation before trade at points P and Q, and after trade by the pair R and T. First let us establish the relationship between q_2/q_1 and p_2/p_1. In Fig. 10 we have the relative price ratios on each axis.

[1] It is obtained by considering a firm's cost equation $C = p_1 A_1 + p_2 A_2$. For a given cost C, this can be expressed as $A_1 = (C/p_1) - (p_2/p_1) A_2$. Hence the slope $a = p_2/p_1$ – ignoring signs and taking the slope relative to the A_2 axis.

We have shown that at commodity price ratio γ_1 there corresponds the factor price ratio α_1. After trade, equilibrium establishes the terms of trade γ_2 and this moves the production towards A in the direction of country I's comparative advantage

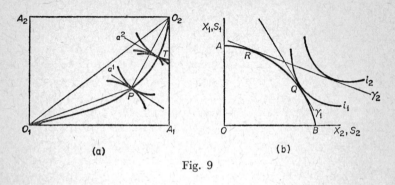

(a)   (b)

Fig. 9

Associated with point R in Fig. 9(b) is point T in Fig. 9(a) which is on a higher isoquant for good 1 but a lower isoquant for good 2. At T the factor price ratio has increased. In other

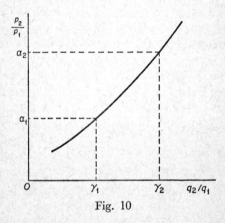

Fig. 10

words, there is a direct association between the commodity price ratio and the factor price ratio as illustrated in Fig. 10. We see that trade results in (i) a higher level of welfare in so far as the economy has moved from indifference curve i_1 to indifference curve i_2 in Fig. 9(b). (ii) Production has moved in favour of the country's comparative advantage, viz. S_1. (iii) Factors have moved out of the production of S_2 and into

34

the production of S_1. (iv) Since good 1 is factor 1-intensive – which is shown by the fact that the efficiency locus lies below the diagonal – the price (return) of the second factor rises relatively to the first. The reason for this is because as industry 1 takes on more of factor 1 its marginal product diminishes, and since a factor is paid its marginal product this also falls. Although the marginal product, and hence the price of factor 2, also falls as more is employed in the production of good 1, it does not fall by the same degree since the intensity of use is less. This means that the relative factor ratio p_2/p_1 is rising. Similarly, in industry 2 the fact that it is factor 2-intensive means that the rise in marginal product and hence price due to the loss of some of A_2 is greater than the rise due to the loss of factor A_1, again resulting in a rise in the relative factor price ratio.

The H–O theorem rests crucially on the concept of factor abundance. There have essentially been two interpretations of factor abundance, each giving rise to slightly different formulations of the H–O model: (i) The *physical* definition, used for example by Samuelson [39, 40], states that if $A_1/A_2 > A'_1/A'_2$ then country I is relatively well endowed with factor 1 and country II with factor 2. (ii) The *price* definition, employed by Ohlin [34] and discussed by Jones [20], is based on relative factor rentals which exist in the two countries prior to trade. It states that if $p_2/p_1 > p'_2/p'_1$ then country I is relatively well endowed with factor 1 and alternatively for country II.

A criticism against both definitions is that they ignore the existence of non-traded goods. Suppose country I is relatively well endowed with factor 1 when considered globally, i.e. for the country as a whole. Further, suppose that the non-traded-goods sector uses most intensively the country's most abundant factor. It is then possible that country I is relatively well endowed with factor 2 when only the traded-goods sector is considered. Furthermore, unless a factor differential is allowed between traded and non-traded goods (which is excluded by assumption of perfect competition in all markets), the physical and price definitions, when referring only to the traded-goods sector, could give opposite interpretations of a country's relative factor abundance.

If demand in each country is assumed identical, the differences in the countries' closed-economy commodity price ratios, which in equilibrium satisfy $\text{MRS}_I = q_2/q_1 = \text{MRT}_I$ and, $\text{MRS}_{II} = q'_2/q'_1 = \text{MRT}_{II}$ respectively, can differ only because of differences in the production possibility boundaries – which, in turn, are different because of the differences in factor endowments in the two countries. This follows readily from our earlier analysis. If demand patterns are the same then the indifference map for country I is identical to that of country II. Now if the production sets were also the same then the equilibrium conditions established in both countries would reflect exactly the same commodity price ratio and there would be little point in trading. The conclusion must be, therefore, 'A difference in the relative scarcity of the factors of production between one country and another is thus a necessary condition for a difference in comparative costs and consequently for international trade,' ([12] p. 278). Under the physical definition differences in demand would not alter this conclusion. But Ohlin argued that demand is to be considered in a discussion of factor abundance ([34] pp. 16–17). Such demand conditions were illustrated by Leontief who introduced the commodity indifference curve into international trade [25]. Employing this technique, Jones demonstrated that demand conditions could be such that the most abundant factor (in a physical sense) commanded a relatively higher rental (price), thus reversing the interpretation of factor abundance [20]. In other words, the indifference maps are so different that the pre-trade price ratios give $p_2/p_1 < p'_2/p'_1$ which suggests that country I is well endowed with factor 2 even though the inequality $A_1/A_2 > A'_1/A'_2$ still holds. It is generally agreed that the physical definition is the more acceptable of the two.

FACTOR REVERSAL

A second problem that has attracted considerable attention in the rigorous formulation of the H–O model concerns factor reversal.[1] The no factor reversal condition was implied in

[1] The consideration of factor reversal arose out of disputes concerning Samuelson's initial paper on the subject of factor price equalisation [39]. The dispute and the error of Samuelson's earlier papers are outlined very well in I. F. Pearce and S. F. James's article

Samuelson's initial paper [39], but was stated explicitly in his 1949 articles ([40] p. 188). If for every factor price ratio the first commodity, say, always employs the first factor intensively, as shown by the rays OA and OB in Fig. 11(a), then we have a situation of no factor reversal. In other words, if, $a_{11}/a_{12} > a_{21}/a_{22}$ for all p_2/p_1, no factor reversal occurs. In Fig. 11(a), no matter what the slope p_2/p_1 the ray OA, representing the relative factor input into commodity 1, is always greater than OB, the relative factor input into good 2. This relationship is also shown in the right-hand quadrant of Fig. 11(b). The corresponding relationship between factor prices and commodity prices is presented in the left-hand quadrant. If, however,

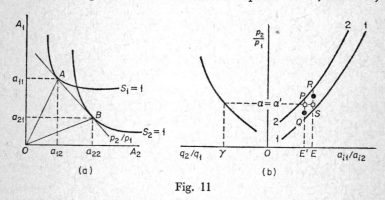

Fig. 11

the factors are more substitutable for at least one of the commodities, then it is possible that at low factor prices the first commodity uses relatively intensively the first factor, but at higher factor price ratios it is the second commodity that uses the first factor relatively intensively. This implies that at some factor price ratio, $(p_2/p_1)^*$, the intensity of the respective factors employed in the production of the two goods reverses [15]. In other words, for some p_2/p_1 we have $a_{11}/a_{12} > a_{21}/a_{22}$ and for others $a_{11}/a_{12} < a_{21}/a_{22}$, the point of factor reversal occurring when for a particular p_2/p_1 – which may or may not be unique [16] – $a_{11}/a_{12} = a_{21}/a_{22}$, as represented by the ray

'The Factor Price Equalisation Myth', *Review of Economic Studies*, XIX (1951–2) 111–20, which also foreshadowed much of the later discussion. It is known that the problem had been looked into as early as 1933, for example by A. P. Lerner, besides others in the years prior to 1948.

OC in Fig. 12(*a*) and the point R in Fig. 12(*b*). It can be seen from the diagrams that if the isoquants intersect only once there will be no factor reversal. If they intersect more than once, factor reversal occurs.

A point to remember in the discussion of production is that reference to countries is unnecessary, and no country has been referred to in the above discussion. The reason for this is that production functions are identical the world over. This means that Figs. 11 and 12 refer equally well to country II as they do to country I; the differences lie in the factor abundances and the factor price ratios.

The problem of having an appropriate definition of factor

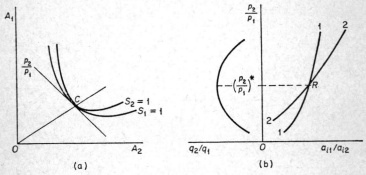

Fig. 12

intensity came to the forefront of discussion following Leontief's test of the H–O model [26]. Leontief appeared to show that the U.S.A. exported relatively labour-intensive goods and imported relatively capital-intensive goods. Since the U.S.A. is normally considered relatively well endowed with capital (in a physical sense), Leontief's results appeared to illustrate the complete opposite of the H–O prediction. A number of theoretical explanations have been put forward to account for this paradox: (i) Leontief considered a bilateral relationship in what is really a multilateral trading system. (ii) Demand was excluded, and to infer that Leontief's results are inconsistent with the H–O theory would possibly be true if the physical definition is considered appropriate. (iii) Ellsworth argued that if *all* inputs are not considered – in particular land, which was excluded by Leontief – this violates the identity of production

38

functions and could explain Leontief's paradox. (iv) The presence of factor reversal along with the fact that Leontief considered not imports but import substitutes. Under identity of production functions and no factor reversal, imports and import substitutes will use the same factor relatively intensively, but with factor reversal this is no longer necessarily true. Investment in human capital which results in the labour inputs being different in the two countries. It is clear from these explanations that it is uncertain precisely how 'robust' the H–O model is under any violation of its assumptions.

Before looking further into factor reversal we must justify such a consideration. In other words, we must ask whether the occurrence of factor reversal is 'pathological' as Samuelson first claimed ([40] p. 188, n. 1), or whether it is a common occurrence. There is a tendency for economists when thinking of production to have in mind a Cobb–Douglas production function, i.e. for the ith commodity:

$$\left. \begin{aligned} S_i &= S_i(A_{i_1}, A_{i_2}) \\ &= \gamma_i A^{\alpha_i}_{i_1} A^{\beta_i}_{i_2} \end{aligned} \right\} \quad (i = 1, 2). \tag{5}$$

This has some important implications in the present context. The most important is that the elasticity of substitution between inputs is unity and this is true of *all* commodities. But it was indicated above that isoquants will intersect more than once if factors are more substitutable in one commodity than in the other. Under the assumption of Cobb–Douglas production functions this is ruled out. This means that factor reversal is ruled out, by assumption.

Arrow, Chenery, Minhas and Solow therefore considered an alternative functional form (e.g. [31]). The function they obtained from empirical evidence, which fitted the data adequately, has become known as the constant elasticity of substitution production function (CES). It has the form:

$$S_i = \gamma_i [a_i A^{-\rho_i}_{i_1} + \beta_i A^{-\rho_i}_{i_2}]^{-1/\rho_i} \quad (i = 1, 2). \tag{6}$$

The name it has reveals its important feature, viz. the elasticity of substitution between the inputs, σ, is constant; in fact $\sigma_i = 1/(1 + \rho_i)$ for the ith commodity. The authors showed that this functional form fitted many industries reasonably well and concluded, firstly, that a CES production function is more suitable than a Cobb–Douglas; and secondly, that the elasticity of substitution differs from industry to industry, i.e. $\sigma_i \neq \sigma_k$ for goods i and k. In other words, one good substitutes factors more readily than another, resulting in the isoquants intersecting more than once, and hence exhibiting factor reversal.

There is, however, a tendency to exaggerate the significance of factor reversal. The presence of factor intensity reversal must be combined with the knowledge of both countries' factor endowment ratios. Consider the situation illustrated in Fig. 13. $E' = A'_1/A'_2$ represents the factor endowment ratio of country II, E_1 and $E_2 (= A_1/A_2)$ denote two alternative factor endowment ratios for country I. If E' and E_1 are

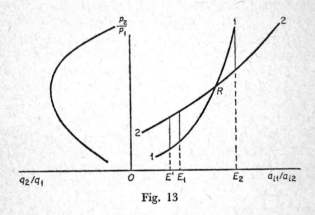

Fig. 13

operative, then to all intents and purposes the condition of no factor reversal can be invoked and all conclusions based on this assumption will hold. If, however, E' and E_2 are operative, then the assumption of no factor reversal is decidedly violated and the conclusions which follow from it are invalid.

The point to emphasise is that the condition of factor reversal is only important when the countries' factor endowment ratios are sufficiently divergent to place them on opposite sides of the factor reversal point. Two developed countries or two developing countries trading are likely to have similar factor endowment ratios and are likely to be on the same side of the factor reversal point. It is unlikely that a developed and developing country, if trading, will have similar factor endowment ratios, and in this context factor reversal considerations are important. This is a consideration to bear in mind when comparing a customs union of developed countries or developing countries compared with one formed from both developed and underdeveloped countries. However, these statements are empirical and can only be established by econometric investigation.

FACTOR PRICE EQUALISATION

A corollary to the H–O theorem is what has become known as the factor price equalisation theorem. Under the assumptions of given factor endowments and their complete immobility internationally, trade theorists have been concerned with the relationship between factor prices in two countries under free trade (i.e. with countries having a common commodity price ratio). The theorem was first outlined by Heckscher [12] and Ohlin [34] and since then has been analysed particularly by Samuelson [39, 40], Pearce [35] and McKenzie.[1] The theorem can be stated as follows:

P.5. Free international trade will equalise relative commodity prices which in turn will equalise relative factor prices in both countries.

The two sufficient conditions for establishing the logical truth of this theorem within the assumptions of the H–O model laid out above, are (i) complete diversification, so that both before and after trade some output of both commodities is produced; and (ii) no factor intensity reversal. In terms of Fig. 11(b), country I's demand is such that its production combination lies somewhere between R and S, both before

[1] The list is immense. Some of the more important ones other than those cited in the text are: A. P. Lerner, 'Factor Prices and International Trade', *Economica*, xix (1952) 1–15; I. F. Pearce and S. F. James, 'The Factor Price Equalisation Myth', *Review of Economic Studies*, xix (1951–2) 111–20; P. A. Samuelson, 'Prices of Factors and Goods in General Equilibrium', *Review of Economic Studies*, xxi (1953) 1–20; L. W. McKenzie, 'Equality of Factor Prices in World Trade', *Econometrica*, xxiii (1955) 239–57; I. F. Pearce, 'A Further Note on Factor-Commodity Price Relationships', *Economic Journal*, xlix (1959) 725–32; the symposium in *International Economic Review*, viii (Oct 1967).

and after trade. (If it was at point R it would be specialising in commodity 2 and if it was at point S it would be specialising in commodity 1.) Similarly for country II, which produces combinations of S'_1 and S'_2 in proportions along PQ. Trade brings about common terms of trade, $\gamma = q'_2/q'_1$, which establishes equality in relative factor prices $\alpha = \alpha'$, and the proportion of S_1 and S_2 can be read off from where this cuts RS and PQ. Comparing the crosses with the dots it can be observed that trade has meant that both countries move in the direction of their comparative advantage.

Early discussions of the theorem were concerned with specifying explicitly these two sufficient conditions. The fact that (i) and (ii) together are sufficient but not necessary can be demonstrated as follows. Suppose factor reversal is present but both countries are on the same side of the factor reversal point such that their factor endowments 'overlap', as shown by E_1 and E' in Fig. 13. In this instance the presence of factor reversal is irrelevant, and trade will equalise relative factor prices so long as specialisation does not occur. Furthermore, as Johnson illustrates [16], if there are two or more factor reversals there may still be a tendency towards factor price equalisation. However, complete equality will be prevented by at least one of the countries specialising.

The literature has now moved in the direction of considering what effect more factors, more commodities and more countries have on the conclusions of the model. Johnson, for example, has argued that the introduction of a third commodity influences the *possibility* of factor price equalisation. He argues that, if the factor ratio of the third commodity lies between the first two, this will not alter the range for which the factor price equalisation can occur. This can be seen from Fig. 11(b). If a factor intensity curve is drawn between 1–1 and 2–2, then the 'overlap' between PQ and RS is unaffected. However, if it is above or below it will increase the range and the likely occurrence of factor price equalisation. He concludes: 'The larger the number of goods relative to the number of factors the more likely is free trade to lead to factor price equalisation' ([19] p. 288). Pearce, on the other hand, presents two somewhat opposing arguments: (i) An increase in the number of commodities, with only two factors, increases the likelihood of factor reversal ([35] p. 484). (ii) The greater the number of commodities over the number of immobile factors, the greater is the probability of factor price equalisation ([35] p. 352). The introduction of a third factor has important implications on the pure theory of trade, but advanced techniques are required to deal with these. The specialist should at least consider one treatment, e.g. Pearce [35]. It is to be observed that statement (ii) does not specify the number of (immobile) factors. It is also to be emphasised, as these statements make clear, that the propositions are probabilistic in nature. In the symposium on this topic[1] the most general formulations were argued by McKenzie, Pearce and Samuelson.

There has been undue emphasis on the factor price equalisation theorem, and in particular on the $2 \times 2 \times 2$ version which is not appropriate in the multilateral, many-commodity and many-factor world of which we are hoping to come to an understanding. It has become more of a doctrinal dispute and its increased abstractness has not taken the issue to a particularly useful conclusion. What has arisen from the discussion is the dependence of many statements and conclusions on empirical evidence which, until recently, has been almost non-existent. The discussion has consequently led to a growth in the empirical testing of both the H–O theorem and the factor price equalisation theorem.

[1] *International Economic Review*, VIII (Oct 1967).

4 Growth and Trade

Classical literature was very much concerned with a country's wealth by means of international trade – in other words, with the effect of trade on economic growth and development. In the post-Second World War period, the theoretical literature has been largely concerned with the effect of growth on international trade, rather than the converse. Interest in this second direction of causation arose from considerations given to the secular dollar shortage, which led to Hicks' important inaugural lecture [13]. The classical direction of causation has also returned the attention of economists to a concern for the problems of developing countries. It is helpful, therefore, to divide this section into two parts.

EFFECTS OF GROWTH UPON INTERNATIONAL TRADE

Under this heading there have been two principal issues: (i) the effects of growth on the terms of trade; and (ii) the effects of growth – via its effect on trade – on economic welfare. We shall return to (ii) in Section 5 below, on 'Welfare and Trade', and shall consider here only the first.

A large proportion of the literature has been concerned with the concept of growth and technological progress, and it has attempted to clarify what is meant by these terms and to derive their implications. This is true of economics generally as it is of international trade analysis in particular. Hicks, in his inaugural lecture, defined neutral technical progress as that which increases the productivity of all industries in a country uniformly. Technological progress favouring the commodity the country exports is referred to by Hicks as export-biased technological progress, whilst import-biased technological progress favours the commodity which is the country's import substitute. Hicks' central proposition is:

P.6. A country which has neutral technological progress, the other country remaining unchanged, will cause the terms of trade to move against itself. ([13] (1959), p. 69)

He argues as follows. A uniform increase in the productivity of all industries in country I will leave relative prices unaffected. But an increase in productivity shifts the production boundary outward since the same factor endowments can now produce more of all goods. Therefore, real income has increased, and this increase in real income will have some effect on country I's demand for country II's exports. If, to begin with, both countries were in balance, then this increase in productivity in country I alone will mean, normally, an increase in country I's demand for country II's exports. The result is a deficit for country I and a surplus for country II. To re-establish equilibrium on the balance of payments, import prices must rise relative to export prices. (In terms of Fig. 6, this means that there must be a movement in the terms of trade to the left to OE.) However, this is the condition for an unfavourable movement in the terms of trade from the point of view of country I.

Alternatively, if technical progress is neutral in both countries the terms of trade will move in favour of the country which is growing the least. Hicks also concludes that the terms of trade will move against the country with export-biased technological progress, and this unfavourable movement is greater than under neutral technical progress. This is because the productivity effect supplements the consumption effect in that export prices are reduced. This favours country I's exports and results in an even greater unfavourable movement in the terms of trade. With import-biased technological progress the terms of trade will move in the country's favour ([13] (1959) pp. 73–5). Although Hicks' article has been criticised strongly on many of its points, it must not be forgotten that it was a most penetrating analysis, and the criticisms have arisen more from its importance than its deficiencies.

The major criticisms and developments have arisen from Johnson [15, 17], MacDougall, Mishan, Corden [6], Asimakopulos and Bhagwati [2, 4] amongst others. This later literature has defined neutrality as an increase in the output of all goods in the same proportion.[1] A further problem is the change in nomenclature which has occurred with Johnson's alternative [17] gaining general acceptance. Economic expansion has both a production effect and a consumption effect – Hicks could neglect demand because of his Ricardian assumptions. To assess the effects of growth we take importables S_2, as numeraire (Fig. 14). In the free trade equilibrium for country I production is

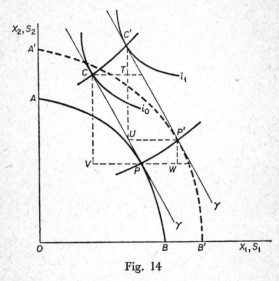

Fig. 14

at point P and consumption at point C on indifference curve i_0. CVP denotes the 'trading triangle' with VP representing the exports of commodity 1, CV the imports of commodity 2, CP the hypotenuse of the trading triangle; γ is the equilibrium terms of trade. Growth is considered as an expansion of the production set, from OAB to $OA'B'$. At constant terms of trade, the new production equilibrium is at P' and the new consumption equilibrium is at C'. In this case the trading triangle is $C'UP'$. At constant terms of trade, PP' denotes the production expansion path and CC' the consumption expansion path due to growth.

[1] Hicks contends that this is not the 'right' generalisation of his definition when increasing costs are allowed. See his 'A Further Note on "Import Bias" ' in his *Essays* ([13] (1959) p. 254).

But how do we know what effect such growth has on the terms of trade? The trading triangle CVP is such that the balance of payments is in equilibrium, i.e. $B = q_1 X_1 - eq'_2 X_2 = 0$. After growth, importables have increased in production by $P'W$ whilst the demand has increased by $C'T$. If the expansion in production outstrips the expansion in consumption, i.e. if $P'W > C'T$, there will be a decrease in the demand for imports, and the terms of trade will tend to move in favour of country I (unless country II's offer curve is infinitely elastic). This is the essence of Johnson's analysis [15] and the alternative treatment given by Corden [6].

Growth which increases the production of exportables, S_1, in greater proportion than importables, S_2, is referred to as

TABLE 1

Consumption		Production	
Consumption effect	Income elasticity	Production effect	Production elasticity
Ultra-pro-trade-biased	$E_{1Y} < 0$	Ultra-anti-trade-biased	$S_{1Y} < 0$
Pro-trade-biased	$E_{2Y} > 1$	Anti-trade-biased	$S_{2Y} > 1$
Neutral	$E_{2Y} = 1$	Neutral	$S_{2Y} = 1$
Anti-trade-biased	$0 < E_{2Y} < 1$	Pro-trade-biased	$0 < S_{2Y} < 1$
Ultra-anti-trade-biased	$E_{2Y} < 0$	Ultra-pro-trade-biased	$S_{2Y} < 0$

pro-trade-biased growth (export-biased growth). If importables are an inferior good in production, then growth will decrease the production of importables giving rise to ultra-pro-trade-biased growth (ultra-export-biased). If the production of importables increases in greater proportion than exportables, growth is anti-trade-biased (import-biased); and if the production of exportables decreases, growth is ultra-anti-trade-biased (ultra-import-biased). Similar biases arise on the consumption side. For example, if growth causes a greater proportionate consumption increase in importables, X_2, this is pro-trade-biased (export-biased). These biases are summarised in Table 1 along with their elasticities. E_{1Y} and E_{2Y} denote the income elasticity of demand for commodities 1 and 2 and refer to the proportionate increase in demand for the commodity due to the proportionate increase in real income (measured in terms of good 2). Similarly, S_{1Y} and S_{2Y} refer to the production elasticities and are the response of production due to growth.

By considering both effects, at constant terms of trade, the new hypotenuse of the trading triangle can be compared with that before growth to obtain the net effect. However, the net effect is not usually specific. Johnson concludes: 'If both shifts [i.e. in production and consumption] are in the same direction or one is neutral, the combined effect is clearly pro-trade-biased or anti-trade-biased. If, however, the two shifts are biased in opposite directions, the net effect cannot be simply assessed' ([17] (1968) p. 286). The conclusion follows from the following formula used for deriving the overall effect of economic expansion, The effect is pro-trade-biased, neutral, or anti-trade-biased according to:

$$b_C + \frac{S_2}{X_2} b_P \underset{<}{\overset{>}{=}} 0 \tag{7}$$

where $b_C = E_{2Y} - 1$ and $b_P = 1 - S_{2Y}$ are the consumption and production biases respectively. They are positive for pro-trade bias and negative for anti-trade bias as can be verified by substituting the elasticities in Table 1 into this formula.

An alternative treatment to ascertain the effects of growth on the terms of trade is provided by Pryor [36]. Pryor proves that with a unitary elasticity of demand for both commodities (i.e. $E_{1Y} = E_{2Y} = 1$) and neutral growth on the production side (i.e. $S_{1Y} = S_{2Y} = 1$) – interpreted as a uniform expansion in the production possibility boundary – the effect is a radial expansion of the reciprocal demand curve with respect to the initial terms of trade. That is, in terms of Fig. 15, $DE/OD = K\mathcal{J}/OK$

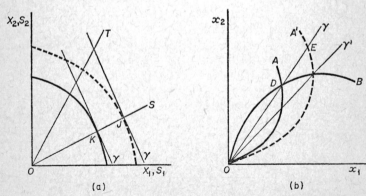

Fig. 15

48

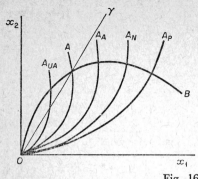

Key:

UA = Ultra-anti-trade-biased
A = Anti-trade-biased
N = Neutral
P = Pro-trade-biased

Fig. 16

is equal to the proportionate increase in the production block ([36] p. 49 and appendix p. 57).

This treatment illustrates explicitly that with neutral economic growth (as here defined) and a uniform expansion in consumption the terms of trade move against the growing country. The reason for this is that imports are the difference between consumption and home production of importables, and the increased production is a smaller proportion than the increased consumption and so the net effect is an increased demand for imports. Net effects other than neutral effects can similarly be obtained. For example, if production is neutral, the production path is along OS, but if consumption is, say, anti-trade-biased the consumption expansion path lies below OT and consequently the radial expansion will be less than under neutral consumption and production effects. It is also clear from this analysis that if both countries grow at the same neutral rate the terms of trade remain unchanged since each offer curve moves radially to the same extent, and that the terms of trade must move against the country with the greatest growth.

The overall consumption plus production effects on the terms of trade are compared in Fig. 16. The only type of net growth which causes the terms of trade to move in favour of the growing country is ultra-anti-trade-biased growth.

The analysis typified by Johnson and Pryor does not consider how growth occurs except on a superficial level, exemplified by statements to the effect that consumption increases arise from increasing population which also changes the pattern of production. Some authors, such as Findlay and Grubert, have attempted to consider more closely the causes of economic expansion. The authors analyse technological progress from the point of view of labour-saving or capital-saving development [8]. With given offer curves and an established trading equilibrium, country I importing S_2, the labour-intensive good, and exporting S_1, the capital-intensive good, the authors argue: (i) Neutral technical progress (i.e. neither labour- nor capital-saving) in S_2 is ultra-anti-trade-biased and neutral technological progress in S_1 is ultra-pro-trade-biased. The movement in the terms of trade will be favourable in the first case and unfavourable in the second. This is because neutral technological progress in S_1 will result in the capital/labour ratio (i.e. A_1/A_2) falling in both industries. If the commodity price ratio is to remain unchanged the factor price ratio p_2/p_1 must fall in order to bring about the increased labour use. But this means that the output of S_2 must fall because now S_1 takes up some of the labour formerly employed in the production of S_2 (note that factor endowments are fixed; it is their utilisation which is changing). In terms of elasticities this condition is $S_{2Y} < 0$ which is ultra-pro-trade-biased according to Table 1. By similar reasoning, neutral technological progress in S_2 will result in a decrease in the production of S_1, $S_{1Y} < 0$, which is ultra-anti-trade-biased. From Fig. 16, the former turns the terms of trade against country I, and in the latter it gives rise to a favourable movement for country I. (ii) Capital-using technological progress in S_2 is ultra-anti-trade-biased and labour-using technological progress in S_1 is ultra-pro-trade-biased, because they both give rise to an increase in the capital/labour ratio resulting in a fall in the production of S_1 in the first case and a fall in the production of S_2 in the second. The movement of the terms of trade will be favourable in the first case and unfavourable in the second. (iii) Labour-using technological progress in S_2 and capital-using technological progress in S_1 have no definite effect, at constant relative commodity prices, on the direction of shift in the output of whichever of the two goods is produced with unchanged technique. Since such technological changes are not, in general, ultra-biased in their effects, the direction of shift in the terms of trade cannot be ascertained on the assumption that neither good is inferior in trade ([8] (1969) p. 238). However, the effects analysed by Findlay and Grubert are only on the production side. Moreover, the literature has concentrated on particular kinds of growth, none of which is 'messy' ([36] pp. 47–8). Also usually excluded are (i) growth in the second country, (ii) problems of multiple equilibria, and (iii) the presence of factor reversal. Not until a 'complete' model is specified can these problems be accommodated. The diagrammatic general equilibrium model is inadequate, as illustrated by Pryor's investigation into 162 possible combinations, which concluded that 115 of them were indeterminate ([36] p. 54).[1]

One cause of economic growth which has had particular attention is the increase in one (or more) of the factor supplies, i.e. an extension of the Edgeworth–Bowley box. This was considered succinctly by Rybczynski [37] and extended by Amano, Guha, Ozawa and Mundell. The Rybczynski theorem can be stated as follows ([37] (1968) p. 74):

P.7. The expansion of one factor input only will raise the output of the good using this factor more intensively and reduce the output of the good using this factor relatively less intensively.

If S_1 is intensive in factor 1 and S_2 in factor 2, and supposing the total endowment of factor 1 increases by dA_1, then, using the H–O model:[2]

$$\frac{dS_1}{dA_1} = \frac{a_{22}}{a_{11}a_{22} - a_{12}a_{21}} \qquad \frac{dS_2}{dA_1} = \frac{-a_{12}}{a_{11}a_{22} - a_{12}a_{21}} \tag{8}$$

Since S_1 is factor 1-intensive, then $a_{11}/a_{12} > a_{21}a_{22}$, i.e. $a_{11}a_{22} - a_{12}a_{21} > 0$. Hence $dS_1/dA_1 > 0$, and $dS_2/dA_1 < 0$, proving Rybczynski's theorem. His argument is illustrated in Fig. 17. O_1A_1 and O_1A_2 represent the original factor endowments and the economy is in equilibrium at point U on the efficiency locus 0_1O_2. Now factor 1 increases by an amount dA_1, factor 2 remaining fixed. Although the isoquants for the production of S_1 are still with reference to O_1, the isoquants for commodity 2 are with reference to the new origin $O*_2$. Draw through $O*_2$ a line

---

[1] Two alternative models which will accommodate most of the conditions simultaneously can be found in Kemp [22] and Pearce [35].

[2] dS_2/dA_1 can be expressed, using $a_{ij} = A_{ij}/S_i$, as

$$\frac{dS_2}{dA_1} = \frac{A_{12}S_2}{A_{12}A_{21} - A_{11}A_{22}}$$

which is the formula given by Bhagwati ([2] (1969) p. 324).

$O*_2U'$ which is parallel to O_2U, U' being the point of intersection with O_1U extended. Since the production functions are assumed to be homogeneous of degree one, the marginal rate of substitution between inputs (i.e. the slope of the isoquant) is the same along any ray through the origin. This means that the marginal rate of substitution in good 1 is the same at U' as it is at U. But also the marginal rate of substitution in good 2 is the same at U' as it is at U. The implication is that the marginal rates of substitution are the same at U' and hence U' is on the new efficiency locus.

Also, under homogeneity of degree one, relative outputs can

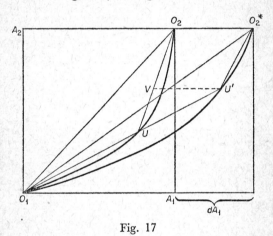

Fig. 17

be measured by radial expansions and contractions. It is clear from Fig. 17 that

$$\frac{O*_2U'}{O_1U'} \quad < \quad \frac{O_2U}{O_1U} \tag{9}$$

and that $O*_2U' < O_2U$, and hence the output of S_2 must be less whilst that of S_1 is greater at U' than at U. The extent of the change is obtained by drawing the horizontal line VU'. Since $O*_2U' = O_2V$ the proportionate increase in S_1 is UU'/O_1U, and the proportionate fall in the production of S_2 is UV/O_2U.

Ozawa has recently supplied a corollary to the theorem, arguing that the production possibility boundary moves in favour of the commodity incorporating the increased factor most intensively. The argument is based on considering the maximum possible outputs in the new situation compared with the initial condition. The theorem has also been extended by Amano who considered the situation when both factors are increasing. He argues that, if factor A_1 is increasing in greater proportion than A_2, then the factor 1-intensive good, viz. S_1, will increase absolutely and the factor 2-intensive good will decrease absolutely if the ratio of the absolute increase in factor 1 to factor 2 exceeds the initial ratio in the production of S_1, i.e. if

$$\frac{dA_1}{dA_2} > \frac{A_{11}}{A_{12}}. \tag{10}$$

Employing this theorem, Rybczynski concludes: if S_1 is an export good, this means that the terms of trade will deteriorate; whilst if it is an import good, the terms of trade must improve ([37] (1969) p. 77). It is clear, however, that Rybczynski's theorem considers only the production effect of growth. If dA_1 denoted the increase in population, then undoubtedly there must also be a consumption effect, and unless this is neutral it is just as important for assessing the net overall effect.

Another proposition which has had some attention is that concerned with *immiserising growth*. This argument has been elaborated largely by Bhagwati ([4] chaps. 13 and 14). As stated above, a growing country will find the terms of trade moving unfavourably. It is possible that the increased welfare from growth is more than swamped by the loss in welfare from an unfavourable movement in the terms of trade. This will arise if a country largely specialises in one good which is an export and which is consumed in small proportion domestically, e.g. a coffee- or banana-producing and exporting country. Whether this proposition is important in practice is an empirical question because it depends upon the probability of certain conditions holding and, in particular, on the closeness of the welfare assumptions to reality.

The arguments outlined have indicated how comparative costs may change in the course of economic growth and development. In particular, we have considered whether the future spread of industrialisation or improvements in productivity will lead to an increase or decrease in the volume and pattern of world trade. It is also possible to consider growth and at the same time maintain certain conditions on the balance of payments, e.g. $B = 0$ ([35] chap. 10).

If we wish to consider the dynamics of such a system, we are concerned with the production expansion path and consumption expansion path over time. This introduces another dimension to the consideration of comparative cost. Nurkse, for example, has pointed out that in considering growth and international trade the relevant consideration is the *incremental* comparative advantage. Although a country's comparative advantage may lie in, say, primary products, there is no necessity to put additional resources into the export sector for the very reason that it would render growth probably ultra-pro-trade-biased or pro-trade-biased, with the result that the unfavourable effects from a deterioration in the terms of trade swamp any favourable effect from growth, i.e. it creates immiserising growth. The consideration therefore is whether the increment in the stock of productive factors should be utilised for developing new export activities or whether it should be used to establish industries catering for home consumption and tending at least initially, on an import replacement policy. These issues are most important but at the same time extremely complex, though not insoluble.

EFFECTS OF INTERNATIONAL TRADE ON GROWTH

Also in the post-war period attention has been drawn to the plight of the developing countries. However, the literature on this direction of causation is less developed theoretically than for the converse outlined in the preceding subsection. Treatment is scant and general. Haberler, for example, argues that international trade, besides inducing a movement along the production possibility boundary (usually in the direction of a country's comparative advantage), also moves the transformation curve outwards owing to indirect dynamic effects. He mentions four dynamic benefits:[1] (i) trade supplies indispensable materials for economic development; (ii) trade is the

[1] G. Haberler, 'International Trade and Economic Development', National Bank of Egypt Fifth Anniversary Commemoration Lectures (Cairo, 1959). An abridged version can be found in G. M. Meier, *Leading Issues in Development Economics* (Oxford U.P., 1964) 352–8.

vehicle for transmitting technical knowledge, ideas, etc.; (iii) trade is the vehicle for the transmission of international capital, particularly from developed to developing countries – this takes the form either of a transfer or foreign aid; (iv) free international trade is the best policy against the possible increase in monopoly power or its beginning, and for an environment conducive to free competition. Of these four, only (iii) has been given any detailed formal treatment.

Although the literature on trade and development is more historical and descriptive, making particular use of case studies, some analytical trends are discernible. It has often been argued that the comparative cost doctrine, being essentially static, is concerned only with resource allocation of a kind which has the country moving along its transformation curve and 'specialising' in the direction of its comparative advantage. Accordingly a country must grow by specialising in the direction of its comparative advantage and trading internationally. This is important from the policy-makers' point of view, who, if they are in agreement with this line of thought will allocate investible funds in accordance with this doctrine.

However, an opposing school of thought, headed by Rosenstein–Rodan, Lewis, Nurkse, Myrdal and others, argues from the point of view of 'growth theory'. These authors stress the interaction among producing and consuming units in a dynamic system [5]. In doing this they emphasise less the general equilibrium aspect and more the sequence of expansion of production and factor use by sector.

The question relevant in this context is: are the gains from trade in conflict with the gains from growth? It is clear from Haberler's arguments that the classical and neoclassical economists considered international trade, as Robertson puts it, as an 'engine of growth'. Growth proposers, on the other hand, consider that another pattern of resource allocation, other than that obtained from comparative cost theory, will lead to an even greater movement outward of the production possibility boundary. The argument can be put as follows. According to the comparative cost theory a country will start its development process from a resource allocation situation in which it is producing only the good in which its comparative advantage lies – or most of its resources are employed in the production of this good. Growth theorists consider the initial resource allocation from the point of view of the multiperiod requirements for production efficiency. The two starting-points, it is argued, are not necessarily the same: in fact, the debate has arisen simply because they consider that the initial points are different. Put differently, if the gains from trade are achieved in each period, this will not lead to a resource allocation which will maximise output over time. The conflict is not as strong as it may appear. A careful consideration of the models, and particularly the assumptions, will reveal that the authors differ as to the significance of basic assumptions.

A number of authors, such as Lewis and Myint, have been dissatisfied with neoclassical analysis – including the H–O theory of trade – because it is inapplicable to the less developed economies. For this reason Myint has attempted to revive Adam Smith's 'vent for surplus' theory of international trade [33]. As an analytical model it is crude but worth considering briefly. The economy concerned is just about to enter into international trade and finds itself at point P inside the transformation curve. A weakness of the theory is in not accounting for the reason why the economy is at point P. The significance is that at P the economy possesses a surplus of productive capacity, i.e. it contains unused resources over and above what it requires to satisfy home demand. In this situation trade is not a means of reallocating *given* resources between S_1 and S_2, but rather of providing a new effective demand for the output of the surplus resources which would have remained unused in the absence of trade. In other words, at the terms of trade PC the economy is stimulated to move to $P'C'$, increasing the production of S_1 without decreasing the production of S_2. This theory implies an inelastic demand for the exportable commodity, S_1 (as shown in Fig. 18 by the consumption expansion path being to the left of OT), and/or a considerable degree of immobility and specificity of resources. (Compare this with the conditions for immiserising growth.) This is in marked contrast to the comparative cost theory ([33] (1968) pp. 322–3).

The 'vent for surplus' theory is applicable to the transition period of a less developed economy which is progressing towards a money and exporting economy and where the market mechanism is beginning to be effective as a means of allocation. It is more than just a historical classification, such as that provided by Rostow's stages of economic growth, for it is

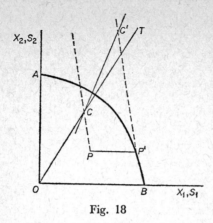

Fig. 18

based on an analytical division. It is saying in effect that the 'vent for surplus' theory will hold in the transition period until the economy is on its transformation curve and is in its expansion phase and responding to market forces. In this case, after the economy has reached P' and C' in Fig. 18, the H–O theory becomes appropriate.

It is impossible in this short space to look into the problems of trade and development, But to give some idea of the considerations raised we shall mention but two topics: (i) increasing returns, and (ii) the dual economy.

The H–O model outlined above, which is so commonly used for analysis, assumes constant returns to scale. However, Hicks in particular has argued that when considering the effect of trade on economic growth, with particular reference to developing countries, increasing returns to scale must be incorporated in the analysis. He says: 'It is impossible to make sense of the phenomena of international trade unless one lays great stress upon *increasing returns* (the economies of large scale).'[1] He further stresses the close connection between increasing returns to scale and capital accumulation, linking this with the problem of the small size of many developing countries, and stressing the limitations of a closed economy.

The effects of trade on growth have also been of concern to those interested in the *dual economy* of some developing countries. Such a developing country is split into a sector concerned

[1] J. R. Hicks, *Essays in World Economics* (Clarendon Press, Oxford, 1959) p. 183.

57

directly with foreign trade, which is a relatively high-productivity capital-intensive sector; the other sector is a low-productivity labour-intensive region. In the former, the technical coefficients (i.e. the a_{ij}'s) are relatively fixed and average income is relatively high; in the latter, factors are combined in variable proportions. Inflows of foreign capital are concentrated in the export sector giving rise to pro-trade-biased growth or ultra-pro-trade-biased growth. This results in fewer opportunities for labour in this sector. As a consequence labour is forced back into the underdeveloped region in the form of disguised unemployment. Technical progress tends to be in the capital-intensive export sector, and labour-saving innovations reduce still further the absorptive capacity of the advanced sector. In other words, the stress of creating an export-oriented economy for the purposes of economic growth and development may promote the advanced sector and retard the backward sector and so cause or increase the duality of the economy.

5 Welfare and Trade

So far we have been concerned essentially with positive economics and have put to one side normative issues. In this section the problems of normative economics are reviewed and consideration is given to the way it has been applied to the problems of international trade. In positive economics it is generally agreed that the conclusions of a theory are to be validated (or falsified) rather than the assumptions. In welfare economics it is important to validate the assumptions rather than the conclusions; moreover, each assumption must be shown to hold in isolation. This partly explains the general concern over the particular welfare criterion adopted. It follows, therefore, that the student who wishes to understand normative issues in international trade – and most of the important problems involve normative issues – must first acquaint himself with the pertinent developments in welfare economics.[1] To see this, consider the following two questions: (i) Can economists pass judgements on international trade policies without invoking ethical judgements about the distribution of income? (ii) Can economists develop useful conclusions on the basis of explicit, generally accepted, ethical norms?

THE GAINS FROM TRADE

Early classical literature did not in fact distinguish positive and normative issues, as illustrated by the arguments against mercantilism and in favour of free trade, or the pamphleteers' discussions on the Corn Laws. The issue of the 'gains from trade' has consistently been debated in the literature. In the classical

[1] A survey of welfare literature up to 1959 will be found in E. J. Mishan, 'A Survey of Welfare Economics, 1939–1959', *Economic Journal*, LXX (1960) 197–256.

theory of comparative costs, country I obtains all the benefit if trade takes place at country II's domestic cost ratio, and vice versa for country II to obtain all the benefit. As implied by Mill's analysis, if the terms of trade lie half-way between each country's domestic price ratio, then the gains from trade will accrue equally to the two countries, which in terms of Fig. 3(*b*) is represented by a terms of trade line whose slope is half-way between that of *AB* and *AD'*. In other words, the terms of trade are an index of a country's gain from trade. This was not explicitly stated by classical economists, but as Viner has pointed out, it is implied in much of their writings. It is also considered today as a viable proposition and lies behind the dictum 'the importance of being unimportant'. In other words, a small country trading with a large country will trade at the large country's domestic cost ratio, and hence gain all the benefit from trade.

The net barter terms of trade (q_2/q_1) have many shortcomings in measuring the gains from trade and there has not been a shortage of alternative measures, e.g. the single factoral terms of trade, which adjust the net barter terms of trade by a correction factor based on the productivity in the export sector; the double factoral terms of trade, which adjust for productivity in both the importing and exporting sectors; and the income terms of trade, which adjust the net barter terms of trade by a factor based on the export volume.[1]

Samuelson, in his classic 1939 article [38], demonstrated that:

P.8. Free trade is superior to no trade.

The sense in which a country is considered better off under free trade is best illustrated for a country which cannot influence its terms of trade. The situation is shown in Fig. 19. Under autarky the effective consumption set coincides with the production set *OAB*, and so the production possibility curve *AB* can also be considered as the consumption possibility frontier. In the case of free trade with international prices

---

[1] These and others are discussed in G. Meier, *International Trade and Development* (Harper & Row, New York and London, 1964) chap. 3.

differing from domestic prices, the terms of trade will be tangential to the production possibility boundary, and at all other points lie outside, as shown by $CP'D$. The line $CP'D$ represents the free trade consumption possibility frontier. Since it lies everywhere to the north-east of the autarky frontier APB (except for a tangency point), the country can have more of all goods with some trade.

Where a country can influence its terms of trade, the free trade consumption possibility frontier is formed by the envelope of the foreign offer curves, which have their origins at various

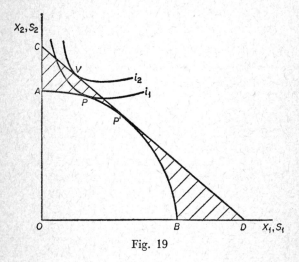

Fig. 19

points on the domestic economy's production possibility boundary, as Fig. 20 illustrates [1]. In this instance the free trade consumption possibility frontier, CD, is concave to the origin but is again north-east of the autarky frontier AB (except for a tangency point). It is in this sense that trade makes a country potentially better off in the Samuelsonian sense – also referred to as holding in the *situation* sense.

This interpretation, however, has lying behind it the 'new welfare economics', which employs the *compensation principle*. It is argued that the gainers could compensate the losers. Debates have arisen as to how many compensations are necessary – Scitovsky's double compensation criterion being generally recognised – as well as whether the compensation is actual or potential. Agreement seems to be reached that it is potential

61

compensations that must be considered. Scitovsky's analysis considers two points which satisfy his double criterion, but Samuelson considers all possible redistributions of income between two situations.

In an attempt to consider all income redistributions Samuelson introduces the utility possibility frontier. To do this he considers a two-person economy, their utility (ordinal) being marked off along two axes as in Fig. 21. To each point on the closed economy possibility curve, e.g. point P on AB in Figs. 19 and 20, there corresponds a utility possibility frontier of the

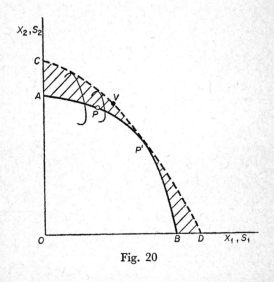

Fig. 20

form $d'dd''$ in Fig. 21. This denotes the varying utility combinations of groups 1 and 2 as they allocate the bundle P by 'ideal-sum transfers' ([41] (1969) p. 175). The envelope curve to all the utility possibility frontiers arising from points on AB is given by pq and is the social utility frontier for the no-trade situation. Similarly $v'vv''$ is a utility possibility frontier for the commodity bundle V on CD in Figs. 19 and 20. The corresponding social utility frontier for the free trade situation is ef. Since the social utility frontier for free trade lies everywhere to the north-east of the no-trade social utility frontier, and compensations take place along the social utility frontiers when production is assumed variable, free trade is superior to no trade for all income distributions [41].

In an analogous argument Samuelson demonstrates that the social utility frontier for some trade is north-east of the frontier for no trade, hence establishing the proposition:

P.9. Some trade is superior to no trade.

As Bhagwati emphasises ([4] p. 155, n. 2), this is not to be read as *any* trade is better than no trade. The reason is that any trade (excluding free trade) is a sub-optimal state, and so is no trade. The theory of second best (see p. 65 below) indicates

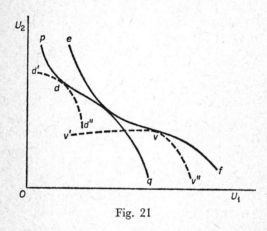

Fig. 21

that it is not possible to rank uniquely, for all income distributions, two sub-optimal states.

An alternative technique is used to compare the utility-wise ranking of free trade and no trade, or restricted trade and no trade. In Fig. 19 the autarky ordinal welfare is given by indifference curve i_1 which is tangential to the production possibility boundary AB at P, and satisfies $\mathrm{MRS_I} = q_2/q_1 = \mathrm{MRT_I}$. With free trade and a foreign price different from the domestic price, utility rises to that indicated by i_2. This increase in welfare arises from two sources. There is a consumption effect due to relative prices being different, and a production effect arising from greater specialisation in the direction of the country's comparative advantage. Employing this approach, Kemp has proposed the following proposition:

P.10. Restricted trade is superior to no trade.

This has been criticised on the grounds that 'restricted' is not any restriction but only for tariffs, quotas and exchange restrictions, if interpreted as Kemp initially formulated it.[1] If compensations are allowed, then any compensated restricted trade is superior to no trade ([4] pp. 155–9).

It is clear that the majority of propositions outlined in this section do not concern actual free trade or actual restricted trade but rather the situation of compensated free trade or the situation of compensated restricted trade compared with the situation of no trade. Accordingly a Bergson social welfare function is still required to decide on actual compensations and income distributions, since the opening-up of trade will always make some people worse off and others better off than they were in the no-trade situation, and so the Paretian condition for a welfare increase cannot be met.

The utility-wise ranking approach also enables us to clarify the argument of immiserising growth, besides the welfare effect of a movement in the terms of trade. If the terms of trade in the post-growth situation are such that the country is consuming on a higher (lower) indifference curve than under autarky (or any other policy), then welfare has increased (decreased) as a consequence of growth. However, we are interested in the question as to under what conditions welfare will increase, decrease or remain unchanged. There is no ready answer. Such solutions that are put forward are very much dependent upon the structure of the model set up by the authors. Employing a simple model ([35] chap. 10) we can say that growth will turn the terms of trade against the growing country in the case where we have stable static equilibrium. But this does not enable us to say that welfare will increase until we can ascertain the value of certain parameters, e.g. marginal propensities to consume and elasticities. An alternative model, with a somewhat different result, can be found in Bhagwati's paper [2], and Kemp ([22] chap. 4.4.), but here again the problem is one of obtaining estimates of the elasticities before any conclusions can be made.

[1] M. C. Kemp, 'The Gain from International Trade', *Economic Journal*, LXXII (1962). See also [22] chap 11.

WELFARE AND DOMESTIC DISTORTIONS

A large part of the literature on trade and welfare has considered the benefits that accrue to a single country when it is in a pre-existing state which far from satisfies the Pareto conditions, and the country wishes to pursue a policy or policies which either relax the constraints or increase them. It is clear that this is the most common state of affairs, and the fact that the theoretical literature has focused on this rather than on the 'ideal' state indicates the economist's desire to tackle policy issues as best he can. The whole discussion comes under the heading of the *theory of second best*.

Meade first explicitly put the argument somewhat as follows ([29] vol. II, chap. 7). Suppose there are ten conditions necessary for a Pareto-optimal solution, but owing to a number of distortions such as taxes, monopoly elements, external economies, etc., only six are satisfied. Suppose now that some policy can remove one particular distortion, bringing marginal values and costs into line, the others remaining unchanged. Then the conclusion of the theory of second best is that economic welfare does not *necessarily* increase, but may diminish. The welfare situation will necessarily improve only when all four distortions are removed simultaneously. From Lipsey and Lancaster's generalisation of second-best theory[1] we have the following important proposition:

P.11. To each set of constraints there corresponds a second-best optimum.

For example, consider one situation of unemployment along with a balance of payments deficit as against a situation of full employment with a balance of payments deficit. The welfare level reached from applying a policy in the first case is not necessarily the same as in the second, for the same policy. It may be that, in the first case, while correcting the deficit employment is created, whilst in the second unemployment is created which leads to a loss in welfare greater than the gain from increased trade.

It is with proposition 11 in mind that each structural model

[1] R. G. Lipsey and K. Lancaster, 'The General Theory of Second Best', *Review of Economic Studies*, XXIV (1956–7) 11–32.

must be reviewed, because alternative structures have different constraints and therefore different second-best optima. Many conflicting statements that appear in the literature are accordingly not actually in conflict at all because the authors have in mind a different economic structure.

Different structures are most apparent in the recent discussions of distortions and their effect upon trade ([4] chaps. 11 and 14; [18]). Distortions can be classified as (i) domestic, in which case under free trade the equilibrium conditions are $\text{MRS}_I \neq q'_2/q'_1 = \text{MRT}_I$, and (ii) distortions in world markets, in which case $\text{MRS}_I = \text{MRT}_I \neq q'_2/q'_1$. A distortion in the commodity market has the effect of raising the market price of the

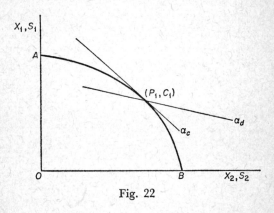

Fig. 22

commodity in which the distortion occurs above its opportunity cost, e.g. under monopoly the good is priced at average cost which exceeds marginal cost. In fact, the relevant marginal cost is marginal *social* cost, and distortions can arise causing marginal private and marginal social costs to diverge, as in the case of external economies and diseconomies. The effect is shown in Fig. 22. In the closed-economy situation production and consumption are at (P_1, C_1). We shall suppose, as we have done so far, that country I has a comparative advantage in good 1. As we argued in Section 2, this is indicated by the slope of the transformation curve at point P_1, and is given by a_c in Fig. 22. The effect of a distortion in the market for commodity 1 is to raise its price; therefore, the ratio q_2/q_1 will fall. This distorted domestic price ratio is given by a_d, and the degree of the distortion is given by the angle between a_c and a_d.

66

Now let trade open up at the international free trade ratio γ, as shown in Fig. 23. Suppose it has the effect of moving production to P_2, i.e. in the direction of the country's comparative disadvantage and resulting in a consumption pattern given by C_2 on indifference curve i_2.[1] By a suitable construction, consumption could equally have occurred on a lower indifference curve than that of i_1 rather than as drawn below. But it is sometimes argued that because there is a domestic distortion in good 1 its domestic production is reduced by free trade as shown by the movement from P_1 to P_2. Accordingly the argument concludes that imports of good 1 should be taxed. The imposition of a tariff on imports (see below, Section 6) will therefore raise the price q_1 to domestic consumers, and this

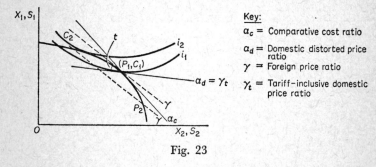

Fig. 23

means that the ratio q_2/q_1 will fall. If protection is taken to be a return to production at P_1 and to compensate for the domestic distortion, then the tariff-inclusive domestic price ratio is γ_t which is equal to a_d, and the appropriate tariff rate is given by the angle between γ (passing through $(P_1 C_1)$) and γ_t ($= a_d$). The effect of the tariff is a production gain but a consumption loss, and in Fig. 23 the consumption loss exceeds the production gain. In other words, the post-tariff level of welfare is less than the free trade level even though that causes a production movement in the direction of a country's comparative disadvantage. This is not a necessary result; the post-tariff welfare level could have increased, which would suggest that protection was bene-

[1] This interpretation given by Johnson [18] does presuppose the physical definition of factor endowment, and hence comparative advantage, for under the price definition the pre-trade (distorted) price ratio would imply that the movement was in favour of the good in which the country had a comparative advantage.

ficial according to ordinal-wise ranking. We can put this result in terms of a proposition:

P.12. It is possible that free trade, even in the wrong direction (i.e. exporting the good for which the country has a comparative disadvantage), *may* lead to a higher welfare level than that accorded to it by protection – which is designed to correct the distortion.

Analysing the situation when free trade leads to a movement in the direction of a country's comparative advantage and comparing this with the situation when an export or import subsidy is imposed to correct the distortion, again results in an indeterminate effect on welfare [18].

Another domestic distortion, considered particularly by Haberler [11] and later by Johnson [18], is factor immobility and price rigidity. Haberler considers two situations: (i) immobility of factors combined with flexibility of factor prices; and (ii) downward rigidity of factor prices, with or without factor mobility. It will be recalled that the H–O model assumes complete mobility internally and so immobility of factors is a direct violation of this condition. However, Haberler shows that this is not a crucial violation so long as there remains complete flexibility of factor prices. The reason for this is that prices will still reflect the opportunity cost of the factors to society and there is no violation of the first-order Pareto conditions for a first-best solution. In this instance there is no domestic distortion, and to present a protectionist policy to overcome the (supposed) distortion arising from factor immobility will simply introduce a distortion in the foreign market which is unjustified.

On the other hand, the situation of downward rigidity of factor prices does introduce a domestic distortion and prevents prices reflecting the opportunity cost of the factors to society. Although the analysis differs depending upon the interpretation of factor price rigidity, the conclusion is still reached that it is factor price rigidity and not factor immobility which is crucial to considerations of welfare differences.

A factor market which has been particularly discussed is the labour market. A distortion in the factor market raises the return to the factor used most intensively in the commodity in which the country has a comparative advantage above the factor's marginal productivity in the rest of the economy. Two reasons have been advanced for such a distortion, both referring to the labour market and both used to favour protection of industry: (i) the earnings of agricultural labour exceed its marginal productivity there, e.g. Lewis has argued,[1] with reference to underdeveloped countries, that labour is paid its average product and not its marginal product; (ii) industrial wages exceed agricultural wages by a greater margin than can be accounted for by the higher costs of urban life. The result is twofold: (a) resource allocation is made inefficient which results in the transformation curve being 'pulled in' towards the origin; (b) the market exchange ratio is likely to differ from the social opportunity cost ratio. Many of these domestic distortions have been used as arguments for the interference with international trade, but as Bhagwati and Ramaswami ([4] chap. 11), and Johnson [18] have argued, they are arguments for interference with the domestic market and not the foreign sector.

MEADE AND PEARCE'S APPROACH TO WELFARE

So far we have been concerned with community indifference curves and the new welfare economics which rests on potential compensated welfare. In doing this, economists avoid the problem of income distribution. But is this approach useful from a policy point of view when we know that actual compensations will not necessarily occur and that the income distribution will change as a result of the policy? Meade has attempted to make interpersonal comparisons [29]. He assumes explicitly *marginal-welfare weights*, and in so doing illustrates to what extent and in what manner a policy choice depends upon the distributional weights allotted to the groups (or individuals) by the policy-makers. Moreover, the treatment is quite general, applying for utopian changes as it does for second-best situations. Meade employed this technique to discuss numerous policies concerned with trade and the domestic economy.

[1] W. A. Lewis, 'Economic Development with Unlimited Supplies of Labour', *Manchester School*, xxii (1954) 139–91.

Pearce on the other hand, uses the theorems of revealed preference theory and concludes that the conditions for a welfare gain for a single individual are given by

$$\left.\begin{array}{l} q^0 dx^0 > 0 \\ q^1 dx^0 > 0 \end{array}\right\} \tag{11}$$

where q^0 is the base price set, dx^0 the change in the consumption bundle due to the policy change, and q^1 the price set after the policy change ([35] p. 367). He argues that if the policy is applied in a small enough degree, $q^1 dx^0 > 0$ – which can be expressed in terms of measurable parameters. He then argues that this is also the condition for the community as a whole, but concedes that it is inevitably true that for some individuals $q^0 dx^0_s < 0$ and for others $q^0 dx^0_r > 0$. Within the limitations laid down, this procedure is operational for measuring the gains or losses from various policies, and he employs it throughout his book [35]. Furthermore, like Meade's approach it is general and applies equally for utopian changes as it does for second-best situations.[1]

CONSUMER SURPLUS AND TRADE

Most welfare aspects of trade consider the general equilibrium model alluded to in earlier sections. However, in discussions, particularly on customs union theory (see below, Section 6), partial equilibrium analysis has played a prominent role. In deriving the welfare benefits of a union the concept of consumer and producer surplus is employed. As in Meade's approach, which is based on Fleming's paper [9], it assumes that the marginal utility of income is constant – the argument being that this is a first approximation which is valid in partial equilibrium analysis and if the policy change is small (as for Meade). The purpose of using consumer surplus is the desire to measure the welfare gains and losses. But this concept has well-defined limitations, as Little and Mishan, for example, have pointed out.

A point worth considering in the context of measuring gains

[1] With the advent of the computer this is the most operational approach to welfare that is available to date, and its comprehensive scope is very much in its favour.

and losses is whether the measure is of first order or second order. For any change in price the loss or gain in consumer surplus for an individual is given by $\frac{1}{2}dq_i dx_i$ where dx_i is the change in quantity of the ith good and dq_i the change in price. If, as in the case of consumer surplus, we take the marginal utility of money to be constant, then the loss or gain in consumer surplus taken over all goods is

$$\text{Consumer surplus} = \frac{1}{2}\sum_{i=1}^{n} dq_i dx_i \qquad (12)$$

or in matrix notation to make it comparable with equation (11), $\frac{1}{2}dq.dx$. But this measure is of second order: it involves the product of two changes. Pearce's measure on the other hand is of first order since it only involves the change dx multiplied by the price set. Any policy brings about changes which can be classified into first, second and higher orders. Generally, the first order is of greater magnitude than the second or higher orders. The point to emphasise is that to measure the gain or loss of a policy measure solely from second-order measures is likely to be very misleading. To measure it solely by first order too is misleading but the degree of error is likely to be smaller. This comment is most relevant for the discussion of customs unions. In particular it must be kept in mind that the terms of trade effect of any policy is a first-order measure whilst consumer surplus is a second-order measure.

It must be apparent that a number of techniques have been employed by economists in an attempt to consider, at the very least, qualitative effects on welfare of particular trade policies. Each approach has its own pitfalls but also a contribution to make. There is no 'right' welfare criterion and there is unlikely ever to be one. Unless there is some progress in the theory of income distribution (economic or otherwise), most questions involving normative issues will not be resolved to most economists' satisfaction.

6 Policy and Trade

The history of trade readily reveals that it has rarely ever been free from government policy. Even when one country may have pursued a *laissez-faire* policy, this has not been so of its trading partners. A government, therefore, is interested in knowing how it can affect a country's trade and what its effect is upon a trading relationship when it carries out either a foreign policy or a domestic policy which has ramifications in the external sector. Under this heading we shall discuss tariffs and exchange restrictions, but with particular attention to tariff policy in a number of its facets.

TARIFFS

Tariffs take two forms: (i) non-discriminatory, and (ii) discriminatory – discrimination being either (*a*) by commodity, or (*b*) by country. They are imposed for a variety of reasons which include the needs: (i) to raise revenue; (ii) to correct a balance of payments deficit; (iii) to protect home producers; (iv) to protect a home factor market – particularly labour; and (v) to shift the burden of taxation on to the foreigner.

The imposition of a tariff, t on importables, X_2, raises the domestic price ratio q_2/q_1 above the terms of trade, since $q_2/q_1 = q'_2(1+t)/q'_1 > q'_2/q'_1$. In considering the effect of this, economists have been concerned about the income distribution effects. If an assumption is made that the tariff revenue is not put back into the economy (or that change in income distribution arising from the tariff revenue is self-compensating), the conclusion has been:

P.13.   Distribution effects aside, the imposition of a tariff will improve the real terms of trade for the country imposing the tariff.

The question arises as to whether this result holds when the tariff revenue is used by the government. Meade ([29] vol. II, chap. 10) argues that the government may (i) increase its budget surplus, (ii) increase its expenditure, or (iii) decrease revenue raised by other forms of taxation. In each case the income redistribution associated with each alternative alters the shape of the offer curve. Without any theory of income distribution we cannot say whether this *redistribution effect* on the terms of trade offsets the favourable *tariff effect*. To argue, as Johnson does,[1] that there is no reason to associate a desirable income distribution with a policy which creates a divergence of domestic relative prices from the terms of trade – such as a tariff – because this is a second-best argument, only emphasises the fact that almost all trade policies which are of any interest are all second best. Even leaving income distribution aside, the result only holds if the foreign goods market is stable. Also, it presupposes that the tariff is not prohibitive.

A further discussion which has been pursued concerns the welfare effect of a country imposing a tariff. In establishing this geometrically, use is made of Meade's *trade indifference curves*. These can be considered as a monotone transformation of the community indifference curves (i.e. they preserve ordinal-wise ranking); but, in addition, they take into account the elasticity of substitution in production between S_1 and S_2 [28].[2] These trade indifference curves are labelled T for country I and T' for country II in Fig. 24. Welfare for country I increases for indifference curves above T and for country II for indifference curves below T'. OA is the offer curve for country I and OB the offer curve for country II. At P we have the situation of free trade equilibrium, with terms of trade γ. If country I imposes a tariff its offer curve shifts to OA_t, which denotes the tariff-ridden offer curve. If we assume that country II does not retaliate, then so long as OA_t cuts OB between P and Q country I must move to a higher trade indifference curve and consequently its welfare must increase. Furthermore, since the new equilibrium is at R, country II must be on a lower trade

[1] H. G. Johnson, 'Comparative Costs and Commercial Policy', *Pakistan Economic Journal*, VIII (1958) 29–43.

[2] A geometrical derivation can be found in C. P. Kindleberger, *International Economics*, 4th ed. (Irwin, Homewood, Ill., 1968) appendix C.

indifference curve to T' and consequently at a lower level of welfare as a result of imposing the tariff.

However, even with static stability (as in Fig. 24), if the tariff is sufficiently large to result in the tariff-ridden offer curve cutting OB below Q, then the reduced volume of trade reduces welfare in excess of the gain from a favourable movement in the terms of trade, i.e. the *trade effect* on welfare swamps the *terms of trade effect* on welfare.

Even in the case of retaliation, a country – but not the world – can be better off. This proposition arose from consider-

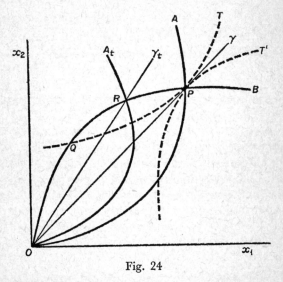

Fig. 24

ations given to Scitovsky's conflicting proposition: in the presence of retaliation it was 'certain' that both countries would finish at a lower welfare than under free trade [39]. This led to discussions contributed to by Kahn, Little, de Graaff and Johnson [14] among others. In demonstrating that Scitovsky's proposition was incorrect, the *optimum tariff* was employed, for example, by Johnson [14] and de Graaff.

It was pointed out above that the imposition of a tariff turns the terms of trade in the country's favour. However, there comes a point where the welfare loss in trade volume is equal and opposite to the terms of trade effect. The tariff giving rise to this is the optimum tariff and satisfies the condition that the tariff-ridden offer curve cuts the foreign offer

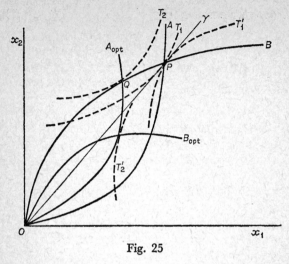

Fig. 25

curve at the point of tangency between the trade indifference curve and the foreign offer curve as shown in Fig. 25. If now the foreign country retaliates and imposes an optimum tariff, it can improve its own position from that at point Q. If it is supposed that optimum tariffs are imposed until an equilibrium is reached, then we have a set of points indicating their reactions. These reaction curves, OR_A and OR_B in Fig. 26, will establish at least one equilibrium – equilibrium being at the intersection

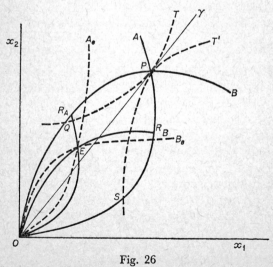

Fig. 26

of the two reaction curves, i.e. at E [14]. The equilibrium does not necessarily leave both countries worse off relative to free trade. If the equilibrium point E lies in the leaf between OB and PQ, then country I gains at the expense of country II. If, however, E lies in the leaf between OA and PS then country II gains at the expense of country I. If it lies anywhere else in the leaf OA and OB, i.e. in the region $OQPS$, then both countries lose relative to free trade. On the face of it, the probability of a welfare increase for one of the participants in a tariff war is small, but the conclusion depends upon the values of a number of parameters.[1]

Two implications can be drawn from the analysis: (i) If both countries are on a lower welfare relative to free trade in the tariff-war equilibrium, then it is possible for both countries to increase their welfare by means of a bilateral trade liberalisation programme. (ii) Since it is possible for at least one country to gain by imposing a tariff policy, then there will exist no *automatic* tendency towards the optimum first-best solution, i.e. free trade. This means that there may exist on the part of some members reticence on agreeing to a trade liberalisation programme.

A debate that has interested nearly all trade economists concerns tariffs as a means of either protecting an industry or protecting a factor of production – usually labour. It is impossible to pursue this discussion here and only a few points will be made, but some of the arguments which have been raised over the past century and a half can be obtained from [3], [11], [18], [24], [43] and [44]. The most important theoretical article on this topic was that of Stolper and Samuelson [44]. The authors argued, in the context of the H–O model, that in going from no trade to free trade, the equalisation of factor prices results in a fall in the relative and absolute share to the scarce factor – in their study, labour. The Stolper–Samuelson theorem states:

[1] The theory of tariff wars is particularly relevant to considerations of the world economy between the wars. It also became topical recently when the American Trade Bill (the Mills Bill) was presented to the Senate; if passed by the House of Representatives and the President, this would have created a tariff war between Western Europe and the U.S.A. The Bill, however, was quashed by President Nixon. (See *The Times*, 23 Nov. 1970.)

P.14. In going from no trade to free trade the real wage of the scarce factor, expressed in terms of any good, falls. Or *prohibitive* protection necessarily raises the real return of the scarce factor.

The converse of this is that prohibitive protection necessarily raises the real return of the scarce factor, and this is true whichever good is taken as numeraire. The authors, in deriving this, assume that the terms of trade are unaffected, i.e. the foreign offer curve is infinitely elastic. Metzler [30] dropped this assumption, arguing that the terms of trade effect could cause the internal price of exportables to increase and hence the return to the country's scarce factor to diminish as a consequence. The theorem has also come under attack by Lancaster. He presents a generalisation of the Stolper–Samuelson theorem, arguing that protection, whether prohibitive or not, raises the real return of the factor in which the imported good is relatively more intensive ([24] p. 199). It will be noted that Stolper and Samuelson, by discussing a prohibitive tariff, avoid the problem of the distribution of tariff revenue. With a non-prohibitive tariff there is a problem as to what the policy-makers do with the tariff revenue. The distribution effect may modify the Stolper–Samuelson conclusion, e.g. if a policy is pursued contemporaneously which is biased in favour of the factor whose real return is diminished by such protection [3].

Arguments concerning protection have arisen from consideration of domestic distortions as outlined in the last section. This is particularly true of infant industry arguments for protection. However, it has been argued by Johnson, Bhagwati and Ramaswami, and others, that a distortion in the domestic market requires a domestic policy and not an interference with international trade. In other words, the presence of domestic distortions – of any kind – is not an argument for protection. And to pursue a protectionist policy will reduce welfare below the maximum obtainable and possibly reduce it below the free trade level. However, these welfare statements are based on the criterion of utility-wise ranking and have lying behind them the principle of potential compensation as outlined in Section 5 above.

This analysis does raise an interesting implication when combined with Tinbergen's analysis on the theory of economic policy. Tinbergen argues that to each policy objective there must correspond a policy instrument. But in trade problems when combined with the domestic economy, it is no longer clear what policy instrument is to be coupled with each policy objective. Furthermore, and most important in the present context, it is not clear that to each policy objective there is one and only one policy instrument. This can only be ascertained in the context of a specific model. Then, and only then, can the degrees of freedom be obtained to carry out a policy objective. For example, in the case of tariffs the policy objective is to correct the balance of payments deficit, and this is done by operating on the import price, which is the policy variable, and the tariff, the policy instrument. (We shall see later that a quota is a policy instrument which operates on the quantity of imports – the policy variable.) But it is not at all clear that the tariff alone is sufficient to correct the deficit, i.e. within the structure whether there is only one degree of freedom. Pearce sets out explicitly a situation in which a tariff (or in his case a quota) is insufficient by itself to correct a balance of payments deficit ([35] chap. 9.4).

CUSTOMS UNION THEORY

Up to this point tariffs have been considered as non-discriminatory. An important development in the theoretical literature is the discussion of discriminatory tariffs and in particular customs union theory. This is defined as 'that branch of tariff theory which deals with the effects of geographical discriminatory changes in trade barriers' ([27] (1969) p. 218).

Prior to Viner's *The Customs Union Issue*[1] it was generally considered that since the formation of a union involved moving 'closer' to free trade, world welfare must have increased. But the discussion of the theory of second best illustrates the fallacy in this argument. Viner also showed the argument to be incorrect. To do this he introduced the concepts of *trade creation* and *trade diversion*. Trade creation depends on opportunity cost and arises from trade created by member countries obtaining imports at a lower cost than at their pre-formation situation.

[1] J. Viner, *The Customs Union Issue* (Carnegie Endowment for International Peace, New York, 1950).

On the other hand, trade diversion entails a movement in trade from a lower-cost source to a higher-cost source, i.e. a movement to a less efficient allocation of world resources. If trade creation exceeds trade diversion, Viner argued, there would be an increase in world welfare. But what about for an individual member? If we suppose that he initially has an optimum tariff with respect to his potential partner, then it would appear that by the very nature of an optimum tariff the country must lose by forming a union – at least on static arguments.

Even so, Viner's analysis concentrates on the production side alone and assumes demand to change in fixed proportion. In so doing Viner fell into the trap of making welfare judgements by considering only the production effect and imputing 'good' to trade creation and 'bad' to trade diversion. But as Lipsey points out [27], the formation of a customs union also has an effect on the world's pattern of consumption. Viner's fixed proportions assumption means that substitution in consumption is ruled out.

Meade's analysis of customs unions[1] follows on from his earlier analysis of trade policy [29]. By assuming the marginal utility of money as constant and the same for all traders, i.e. importers and exporters both before and after tariffs, Meade directs the attention of welfare changes to changes in the *volume* of trade. A net increase in the volume of trade means an increase in welfare. A similar analysis has been employed, e.g. by Johnson, Humphrey and Ferguson, and others, in considering the welfare implications of a customs union. They use a partial equilibrium analysis and make use of the consumer and producer surplus, but in so doing they are considering only second-order measures. This approach also means that welfare assessments are made by considering only the changes in the volume of trade. It also tends to ignore the terms of trade effect of a union, a first-order measure, although Humphrey and Ferguson try to introduce it into their analysis.[2] In all cases the

[1] J. E. Meade, *The Theory of Customs Unions* (North-Holland, Amsterdam, 1956).

[2] The terms of trade effect is explicitly taken into account in the offer-curve treatment of customs union theory, a treatment considered particularly by J. Vanek, *International Trade: Theory and Economic Policy* (Irwin, Homewood, Ill., 1962) pp. 346–59.

tariffs are supposedly marginal and the secondary effects small and so can be neglected on a first approximation. However, this is far from true for the formation of a customs union.

The literature has concentrated attention on the welfare aspects of a union arising from (i) the specialisation of production according to comparative advantage, (ii) economies of scale, (iii) changes in the terms of trade, (iv) forced changes in efficiency due to increased foreign competition, and (v) a change in the rate of economic growth, rather than the effects on economic activity, the balance of payments, or the rate of inflation. But it is apparent that the problem is more dynamic than static, and the static models considered can tell only part of the story.

EFFECTIVE TARIFF RATE

A more recent introduction into the literature, which has implications for all that has been said up to this point, is the distinction between the *nominal tariff* and the *effective tariff*. Early contributions to the discussion of tariff structure came from Barber, Humphrey, Corden [7], Johnson, Basevi, Balassa and others. This analysis gives particular attention to intermediate production which employs inputs which are imported and whose price indicates a tariff. Consequently attention has shifted to considering economic activities rather than final consumption.

The effective tariff rate has been defined in terms of the increase in value added made possible by the tariff structure relative to the situation before any tariffs were imposed ([17] (1969) pp. 285–6). We can make this explicit as follows. Consider the production of commodity 2, an importable. We shall suppose that this uses two basic inputs, A_{21} and A_{22}, and an importable good S_{23}, which is the input of S_3 in the production of S_2. The production function takes the general form, with its associated cost equation:

$$S_2 = S_2(A_{21}, A_{22}, S_{23})$$
$$q_3 = p_1 a_{21} + p_2 a_{22} + p_3 a_{23} \tag{13}$$

with $a_{23} = S_{23}/S_2$ and $a_{ij} = A_{ij}/S_i$ for $i, j = 1, 2$ as before. It is clear from this cost equation that the value added is $v_2 = p_1 a_{21} +$

$p_2 a_{22} = q_2 - p_3 a_{23}$. Now consider the situation when tariffs are imposed on importables S_2 and S_3 and there are no taxes or subsidies elsewhere. The cost equation takes the form:

$$q_2(1+t_2) = p_1 a_{21} + p_2 a_{22} + p_3(1+t_3)a_{23} \qquad (14)$$

and its associated value added is $v'_2 = p_1 a_{21} + p_2 a_{22} = q_2(1+t_2) - p_3(1+t_3)a_{23}$. Consider now the proportion of each input to total cost, e.g. $p_3 a_{23}$ in equation (13) contributes $a_{23} q_2$ to the total cost. Substituting we obtain $v_2 = q_2 - a_{23}q_2$ and $v'_2 = q_2(1+t_2) - a_{23}(1+t_3)q_2$. Hence the effective tariff g_2 is defined:

$$g_2 \equiv \frac{v'_2 - v_2}{v_2} = \frac{q_2[(1+t_2) - a_{23}(1+t_3)] - q_2(1 - a_{23})}{q_2(1 - a_{23})}$$

$$= \frac{t_2 - a_{23}t_3}{1 - a_{23}} \qquad (15)$$

The analysis, however, is very specific. Rigid assumptions are usually made – in particular, that of infinite elasticities. To see the significance of this, consider equation (14). If we suppose no tariff on S_2, the final goods price q_2 remains fixed both before and after the tariff on S_3 because of the infinite elasticity of supply assumption. As a consequence, *all* the effect is shifted on to the value added, v'_2. (This is also true with a tariff on S_2 because its price rises by the full amount of the tariff under this assumption.)

The analysis does, however, give rise to some interesting conclusions, some of which will be only slightly modified once the model is made more realistic. Corden, for example, concludes that (i) it aids in understanding the phenomenon that tariffs escalate with the degree of processing; this results in (*a*) the effective rate always exceeding the nominal rate, and (*b*) it means low or zero protection for raw materials at the bottom of the structure. (ii) A concessionary reduction of a tariff on an intermediate good in order to reduce the protection and increased trade may not in fact have this result. (iii) Arguments on nominal rates increasing with reference to developing countries are misleading; the effective rate is more important.[1] Balassa also substantiates these claims.

[1] A very interesting discussion of this will be found in H. G. Johnson, *Economic Policies Towards Less Developed Countries* (Allen & Unwin, 1967) pp. 170–81.

There is yet much to clarify in this analysis, but its empirical usefulness is one of its advantages.

QUOTAS

An alternative method of restricting trade which has been employed with varying success is that of quotas. The government by imposing quotas restricts imports, which raises the domestic price of importables above the world price by means of competition, and in effect lets price find its own level. As an alternative to restricting the volume of imports to a specified amount, say by the issue of import licences, the government can ration foreign exchange. The choice is more practical than theoretical.

The literature is in general agreement on the proposition:

P.15. Redistribution effects aside, the effects of a quota are the same as the effects of a tariff and of equal magnitude.

Bhagwati, however has recently contended that under very reasonable situations the equivalence breaks down. What is more to the point, arguments which hold under equivalence do not usually hold under non-equivalence of tariffs and quotas ([4] pp. 261–5), e.g. if a quota is economically justified so is a tariff and vice versa. Unless 'economically justified' is defined tautologically, this will not hold when non-equivalence exists. It is also to be noted that proposition 15 excludes any redistribution effects, but it is in this respect that a quota is likely to differ from a tariff.

7 Recent Developments

In conclusion, we shall consider briefly a number of extensions and complications which have arisen, and see if any modifications are in order. In this respect we shall consider the introduction of non-tradeable goods, intermediate and capital goods, and the modifications arising from variable returns to scale.

NON-TRADED GOODS

Non-tradeable goods have already been referred to, but interest in them is fairly recent. Non-traded goods arise largely because of transport costs, and interest in them arises from the fact that their price changes move in a different manner from internationally traded commodities. They were mentioned in the literature by Taussig, Viner and Wilson, but it was once again Meade who explicitly introduced non-traded goods into international trade [29]. However, his conclusion was indeterminate and it was Pearce who pointed out that Meade had not taken full advantage of basic results in micro-economics which allowed qualitative (and, to a certain degree, quantitative) results to be obtained in a not too complicated model. The analysis of basic trade relations including a non-tradeable good has been extended by McDougall, Komiya and Melvin and is fully integrated into Pearce's basic text [35].

The introduction of non-traded goods (i) alters slightly stability conditions in the market for traded goods. (ii) In the context of tariffs it results in the Metzler effect being more likely to be met, because of the substitution effect between traded and non-traded goods – which was excluded earlier. (iii) It is important in the discussion of effective tariff structure because of the substitution between traded and non-traded inputs. (iv) Discussion of economic growth and its relation with trade is made more realistic by the introduction of non-tradeable goods, e.g. growth in the non-traded-goods sector alone will alter the terms of trade between traded and non-traded-goods and as a consequence will create a balance of payments problem. Correction by influencing trade will, in this case, be inappropriate. (v) As discussed earlier, domestic distortions affect trade and the country's welfare. Taxes and subsidies on non-traded goods, therefore, will have an effect on trade which has been generally neglected. (vi) Its introduction will mean that non-equivalence between tariffs and quotas or between taxes on imports or exports is more likely. The introduction of a non-tradeable good, it must be emphasised, is more significant than the introduction of a third commodity. A third commodity is usually a traded good in which case the analysis remains largely unaffected; but the introduction of a non-tradeable good, in particular, introduces a second terms of trade, viz. that between traded and non-traded goods.

INTERMEDIATE AND CAPITAL GOODS

In the discussion on the effective tariff it was indicated that the attention of trade economists has switched to production activities and intermediate production. However, the analysis of the effective tariff rate has been developed from a practical point of view and stands in isolation from the bulk of trade theory. What has been lacking is the introduction of intermediate goods and capital goods in a framework such as the H–O model. A consideration of the U.K. or U.S. input–output matrix will indicate the importance of considering intermediate production and capital goods. They have not been completely neglected in the literature. Intermediate goods have been considered by McKenzie, Jones, Vanek and Kemp [22], whilst capital goods have been considered by Samuelson, Ramaswami and Srinivasan.

It is generally argued by the authors that the introduction of intermediate goods can be absorbed into the H–O framework and that the principal theorems, viz. the Stolper–Samuelson theorem (p. 77) and the Rybczynski theorem (p. 51), carry over with only trivial changes. In other respects the introduction of intermediate and capital goods does make a difference.

The existence of taxes and subsidies on these goods will affect production patterns and hence the type of goods, their price, and the volume of goods traded. Consideration of such goods is particularly relevant for developing countries since the bulk of their imports are intermediate and/or capital goods. Furthermore, the implications of such trade on the growth of developing countries have far greater consequences than the trade of final consumption goods analysed on pp. 54–8 above.

INCREASING RETURNS TO SCALE

Throughout this essay a repeated assumption has been that of constant returns to scale. In making this assumption the analysis has focused on factor *proportions* and output ratios without considering as being important the size of a country's resource endowment or the scale of its productive and trading operations. In particular, all propositions derived in the framework of the H–O model are dependent upon this assumption. In allowing variable returns to scale one must consider economies and diseconomies of scale. These can be either internal or external. In a static world, internal economies would lead to a single producer and are of little theoretical interest. On the other hand, external economies will still allow perfectly competitive conditions to prevail – in that firms are price-takers and there remains complete freedom of entry and exit from the industry – even though marginal costs to the firm are either constant or rising. This may lead to the production point being interior to the production possibility boundary, or to the equilibrium price ratio not being equal to the slope of the production possibility boundary, i.e. $MRS_I = q_2/q_1 \neq MRT_I$, which gives rise to a domestic distortion.

Although some types of economies of scale, such as those analysed by Herberg and Kemp, and Kemp [22], are consistent with perfect competition, this is not true of all types, some of which inevitably lead to some monopoly elements. In this case specialisation in production becomes more likely and this, for one, prevents the equalisation of factor prices, or cuts short the tendency towards factor price equalisation.

8 A Warning: Three Commodities and Three Factors

It was pointed out earlier that with more than two factors the concept of factor intensity breaks down; furthermore, in the section on tariffs it was argued that in going from no trade to free trade the wage of the scarce factor is reduced, but this too is dependent upon the concept of factor intensity. The Rybczynski theorem also makes reference to factor intensity, as do many arguments of the Leontief paradox. Growth has been analysed in a $2 \times 2 \times 2$ world. It is most important for the student to be aware that in the field of international trade the generalisation to more than two goods or two factors reduces the significance of many of the former theorems.

In order to demonstrate this important point, one aspect of trade theory will be dealt with in detail, viz. the Stolper–Samuelson theorem (proposition 14, p. 77 above). The conclusion of this proposition is obtained solely from the assumptions being made. Assumptions are often of a simplifying nature and do not radically alter the problem when they are dropped, but this is generally not true in trade when three or more factors and commodities are considered. The reason for this is that with only two commodities if the output of one increases the other must diminish. This is because with fixed factor endowments when more is used in one industry less must be used in the other and it can never be anything other than this. In other words, cost conditions alone determine which prices rise and which fall, demand determining only the extent.

With three factors and three commodities, however, demand must play its part in determining both the direction and the amount of the change.

Suppose the economy is composed of three commodities and three fixed factors of production.[1] The cost equations are:

$$q_1 = a_{11}p_1 + a_{12}p_2 + a_{13}p_3$$
$$q_2 = a_{21}p_1 + a_{22}p_2 + a_{23}p_3 \qquad (16)$$
$$q_3 = a_{31}p_1 + a_{32}p_2 + a_{33}p_3.$$

We wish to know the relationship between the change in the price of, say, factor 1 due to the change in commodity prices which arises when a country opens up trade. Taking changes and using the conditions that the a_{ij} are, at the going factor prices, the minimum-cost technique, then $p_1 da_{i1} + p_2 da_{i2} + p_3 da_{i3} = 0 (i = 1, 2, 3)$, and we have:

$$dq_1 = a_{11}dp_1 + a_{12}dp_2 + a_{13}dp_3$$
$$dq_2 = a_{21}dp_1 + a_{22}dp_2 + a_{23}dp_3 \qquad (17)$$
$$dq_3 = a_{31}dp_1 + a_{32}dp_2 + a_{33}dp_3.$$

Solving for dp_1 by using Cramer's rule and taking commodity 2 as numeraire so that $dq_2 = 0$, we have:

$$dp_1 = \frac{\begin{vmatrix} dq_1 & a_{12} & a_{13} \\ 0 & a_{22} & a_{23} \\ dq_3 & a_{32} & a_{33} \end{vmatrix}}{|a_{ij}|} \qquad (18)$$

where $|a_{ij}|$ is the determinant of coefficients, a_{ij}.

Before analysing this result let us write down the same result for the two-commodity, two-factor case. Following the same procedure we would get:

$$dp_1 = \begin{vmatrix} dq_1 & a_{12} \\ 0 & a_{22} \end{vmatrix} \Big/ \begin{vmatrix} a_{11} & a_{12} \\ a_{21} & a_{22} \end{vmatrix} \qquad (19)$$

In order to obtain the sign of dp_1 we must sign explicitly both numerator and denominator. Consider the denominator of equation (19); this is $a_{11}a_{22} - a_{12}a_{21}$, but by postulating that commodity 1 is factor 1-intensive, this is positive. But what of the denominator in equation (18)? No such postulation can be made: factor intensity has no meaning, and so we cannot put a sign on $|a_{ij}|$.

This is not all. In equation (19) the numerator is $dq_1 a_{22}$ and

[1] This argument follows that of Pearce ([35] chap. 14).

dq_1 is the only commodity price needed to sign dp_1, i.e. with dq_1 positive dp_1 is positive. But in equation (18) we need to know dq_3 besides, and there is no *a priori* reason for saying that this is positive or negative.

On two accounts therefore we cannot sign the change in dp_1. We could take this demonstration further, but it must be clear to the student that a great deal of uncertainty enters when we go to three factors and three commodities. Had the assumptions been *solely* simplifying, this uncertainty would not have arisen.

This problem arises repeatedly. A look back at equation (8) on p. 51 will reveal that the denominator in both expressions is $|a_{ij}|$. Their signs were determined by appealing to factor intensity, but this is impossible in a three-commodity, three-factor world, and so this theorem too loses its significance.

The lesson to be learned from this section is that the literature has paid too much attention to the $2 \times 2 \times 2$ case. This essay reflects this emphasis in that it surveys the literature, but in conclusion it would urge the student to question all pre-existing results and ask himself whether they still hold when the number of commodities or the number of factors exceeds two. To answer such a question one requires to specify explicitly a model indicating which variables are endogenous and which exogenous; only then will such concepts as factor intensity be shown to be meaningless except in a very restrictive and unimportant sense.

9 Conclusion

The pure theory of international trade has come a long way from Ricardo's comparative cost doctrine, but we are still a long way from explaining many of the trade phenomena which exist in the world today. Part of the reason for this is that trade theory has remained in the realm of comparative statics with little attention placed on dynamics. This is inevitable in such a complicated interrelated system. Trade theory must explicitly take into account non-economic objectives and place trade theory in a larger socio-politico-economic setting if we wish the theory to be of any practical use. In this sense we would be returning to issues which the classical economists knew were important, but with the difference that our value judgements are made explicit, and with a greater understanding of the economic system.

Select Bibliography

[1]   R. E. Baldwin, 'The New Welfare Economics and Gains in International Trade', *Quarterly Journal of Economics*, LXVI (1952) 91–101. Reprinted in R. E. Caves and H. G. Johnson (eds), *Readings in International Economics* (Allen & Unwin, London, 1968) chap. 12.

[2]   J. Bhagwati, 'International Trade and Economic Expansion', *American Economic Review*, XLVIII (1958) 941–53. Reprinted in J. Bhagwati (ed.), *International Trade* (Penguin Books, Harmondsworth, 1969) chap. 13. Also in [4] chap. 12.

[3]   J. Bhagwati, 'Protection, Real Wages and Real Incomes', *Economic Journal*, LXIX (1959) 733–44. Reprinted in J. Bhagwati (ed.), *International Trade* (Penguin Books, Harmondsworth, 1969) chap. 11. Also in [4] chap. 7.

[4]   J. Bhagwati, *Trade, Tariffs and Growth* (Weidenfeld & Nicolson, London, 1969).

[5]   H. B. Chenery, 'Comparative Advantage and Development Policy', *American Economic Review*, LI (1961) 18–51.

[6]   W. M. Corden, 'Economic Expansion and International Trade: A Geometric Approach', *Oxford Economic Papers*, VIII (1956) 223–8.

[7]   W. M. Corden, 'The Structure of a Tariff System and the Effective Protection Rate', *Journal of Political Economy*, LXXIV (1966) 221–37. Reprinted in J. Bhagwati (ed.), *International Trade* (Penguin Books, Harmondsworth, 1969) chap. 12.

[8]   R. Findlay and H. Grubert, 'Factor Intensities, Technological Progress and the Terms of Trade', *Oxford Economic Papers*, XI (1959) 111–21. Reprinted in J. Bhagwati (ed.), *International Trade* (Penguin Books, Harmondsworth, 1969) chap. 14.

[9]   J. M. Fleming, 'On Making the Best of Balance of

Payments Restrictions on Imports', *Economic Journal*, LXI (1951) 48–71. Reprinted in R. E. Caves and H. G. Johnson (eds), *Readings in International Economics* (Allen & Unwin, London, 1968) chap. 15.

[10] G. Haberler, *The Theory of International Trade* (William Hodge, London, 1936).

[11] G. Haberler, 'Some Problems in the Pure Theory of International Trade', *Economic Journal*, LX (1950) 223–40. Reprinted in R. E. Caves and H. G. Johnson (eds), *Readings in International Economics* (Allen & Unwin, London, 1968) chap. 13.

[12] E. Heckscher, 'The Effects of Foreign Trade on the Distribution of Income', *Ekonomisk Tidskrift*, XXI (1919) 497–512. Reprinted in H. S. Ellis and L. A. Metzler (eds), *Readings in the Theory of International Trade* (Allen & Unwin, London, 1950) chap. 13.

[13] J. R. Hicks, 'An Inaugural Lecture', *Oxford Economic Papers*, V (1953) 117–35. Slightly abridged version under title 'The Long-Run Dollar Problem' in R. E. Caves and H. G. Johnson (eds), *Readings in International Economics* (Allen & Unwin, London, 1968) chap. 26. Also in J. R. Hicks, *Essays in World Economics* (Clarendon Press, Oxford, 1959) chap. 4.

[14] H. G. Johnson, 'Optimum Tariffs and Retaliation', *Review of Economic Studies*, XXI (1953–4) 142–53. Reprinted in H. G. Johnson, *International Trade and Economic Growth* (Allen & Unwin, London, 1958) chap. 2.

[15] H. G. Johnson, 'Economic Expansion and International Trade', *Manchester School of Economic and Social Studies*, XXIII (1955) 95–112. Reprinted, with revisions, in H. G. Johnson, *International Trade and Economic Growth* (Allen & Unwin, London, 1958) chap. 3.

[16] H. G. Johnson, 'Factor Endowments, International Trade, and Factor Prices', *Manchester School of Economic and Social Studies*, XXV (1957) 270–83. Reprinted in R. E. Caves and H. G. Johnson (eds), *Readings in International Economics* (Allen & Unwin, London, 1968) chap. 5.

[17] H. G. Johnson, 'Economic Development and International Trade', in H. G. Johnson, *Money, Trade and*

Economic Growth (Allen & Unwin, London, 1964) chap. 4. Also in R. E. Caves and H. G. Johnson (eds), *Readings in International Economics* (Allen & Unwin, London, 1968) chap. 17.

[18]   H. G. Johnson, 'Optimal Trade Intervention in the Presence of Domestic Distortions', in R. E. Caves *et al.* (eds), *Trade, Growth, and the Balance of Payments* (Rand McNally, Chicago, 1965) pp. 3–34. Reprinted in J. Bhagwati (ed.), *International Trade* (Penguin Books, Harmondsworth, 1969) chap. 8.

[19]   H. G. Johnson, 'The Possibility of Factor-Price Equalisation when Commodities Outnumber Factors', *Economica*, xxxiv (1967) 282–8.

[20]   R. W. Jones, 'Factor Proportions and the Heckscher–Ohlin Theorem', *Review of Economic Studies*, xxiv (1956–7) 1–10. Reprinted in J. Bhagwati (ed.), *International Trade* (Penguin Books, Harmondsworth, 1969) chap. 4.

[21]   R. W. Jones, 'Comparative Advantage and the Theory of Tariffs: A Multi-Country Multi-Commodity Model', *Review of Economic Studies*, xxvii (1961) 161–75.

[22]   M. C. Kemp, *The Pure Theory of International Trade* (Prentice-Hall, Englewood Cliffs, N.J., 1964). Also idem, 2nd ed. (1969) under the title *The Pure Theory of International Trade and Investment*.

[23]   K. Lancaster, 'The Heckscher–Ohlin Trade Model: A Geometric Treatment', *Economica*, xxiv (1957) 19–39. Reprinted in J. Bhagwati (ed.), *International Trade* (Penguin Books, Harmondsworth, 1969) chap. 3.

[24]   K. Lancaster 'Protection and Real Wages: A Restatement', *Economic Journal*, lxvii (1957) 199–210.

[25]   W. W. Leontief, 'The Use of Indifference Curves in the Analysis of Foreign Trade', *Quarterly Journal of Economics*, xlvii (1933) 493–503. Reprinted in J. Bhagwati (ed.), *International Trade* (Penguin Books, Harmondsworth, 1969) chap. 1.

[26]   W. W. Leontief, 'Domestic Production and Foreign Trade: The American Capital Position Re-examined', *Economia Internazionale*, vii (1954) 3–32. Reprinted in

J. Bhagwati (ed.), *International Trade* (Penguin Books, Harmondsworth, 1969) chap. 5.

[27] R. G. Lipsey, 'The Theory of Customs Unions: A General Survey', *Economic Journal*, LXX (1960) 496–513. Reprinted in J. Bhagwati (ed.), *International Trade* (Penguin Books, Harmondsworth, 1969) chap. 9.

[28] J. E. Meade, *A Geometry of International Trade* (Allen & Unwin, London, 1952).

[29] J. E. Meade, *The Theory of International Economic Policy*. vol. I, *The Balance of Payments*; vol. II, *Trade and Welfare* (Oxford U.P., 1951, 1955). Also Mathematical Supplements.

[30] L. A. Metzler, 'Tariffs, the Terms of Trade, and the Distribution of National Income', *Journal of Political Economy*, LVII (1949) 1–29. Reprinted in R. E. Caves and H. G. Johnson (eds), *Readings in International Economics* (Allen & Unwin, London, 1968) chap. 2.

[31] B. S. Minhas, 'The Homohypallagic Production Function, Factor-Intensity Reversals and the Heckscher–Ohlin Theorem', *Journal of Political Economy*, LXX (1962) 138–56. Reprinted in J. Bhagwati (ed.), *International Trade* (Penguin Books, Harmondsworth, 1969) chap. 6.

[32] R. A. Mundell, 'The Pure Theory of International Trade', *American Economic Review*, L (1960) 67–110. Reprinted in R. A. Mundell, *International Economics* (Macmillan, London, 1968) chaps. 1–4.

[33] H. Myint, 'The "Classical Theory" of International Trade and the Underdeveloped Countries', *Economic Journal*, LXVIII (1958) 317–37. Reprinted in R. E. Caves and H. G. Johnson (eds), *Readings in International Economics* (Allen & Unwin, London, 1968) chap. 20.

[34] B. Ohlin, *Interregional and International Trade* (Oxford U.P., 1933; rev. ed., 1967).

[35] I. F. Pearce, *International Trade* (Macmillan, London, 1970).

[36] F. Pryor, 'Economic Growth and the Terms of Trade', *Oxford Economic Papers*, XVIII (1966) 45–57.

[37] T. N. Rybczynski, 'Factor Endowment and Relative Commodity Prices', *Economica*, XXII (1955) 336–41.

Reprinted in R. E. Caves and H. G. Johnson (eds), *Readings in International Economics* (Allen & Unwin, London, 1968) chap. 4.

[38] P. A. Samuelson, 'The Gains from International Trade', *Canadian Journal of Economic and Political Science*, v (1939) 195–205. Reprinted in H. S. Ellis and L. A. Metzler (eds), *Readings in the Theory of International Trade* (Allen & Unwin, London, 1950) chap. 11.

[39] P. A. Samuelson, 'International Trade and the Equalisation of Factor Prices', *Economic Journal* LVIII (1948) 163–84.

[40] P. A. Samuelson, 'International Factor-Price Equalisation Once Again', *Economic Journal*, LIX (1949) 181–97.

[41] P. A. Samuelson, 'The Gains from International Trade Once Again', *Economic Journal*, LXXII (1962) 820–9. Reprinted in J. Bhagwati (ed.), *International Trade* (Penguin Books, Harmondsworth, 1969) chap. 7.

[42] K. M. Savosnick, 'The Box Diagram and the Production Possibility Curve', *Ekonomisk Tidskrift*, LI (1958) 183–97.

[43] T. Scitovsky, 'A Reconsideration of the Theory of Tariffs', *Review of Economic Studies*, IX (1942) 89–110. Reprinted in H. S. Ellis and L. A. Metzler (eds), *Readings in the Theory of International Trade* (Allen & Unwin, London, 1950) chap. 16.

[44] W. F. Stolper and P. A. Samuelson, 'Protection and Real Wages', *Review of Economic Studies*, IX (1941) 58–73. Reprinted in J. Bhagwati (ed.), *International Trade* (Penguin Books, Harmondsworth, 1969) chap. 10.